MITAKUYE OYASIN
"We are all related"

Dr. A. C. Ross

Cover Story

The shield on the cover was made by the author. The picture painted on the shield was taken from a dream that Dr. Ross had in 1977. The red and white sections in the lower half of the shield represent two different ways of thinking. Red for American Indian and white for the white man. The bird represents the Wakinyan Oyate (Thunder Beings). The bolt of lightning which is the symbol of the Wakinyan Oyate separates the bird from the heavens. One year after this shield was made, Dr. Ross synchronistically came across brain hemispheric research (see pp 14-18 for details). He soon discovered that right hemispheric modes of thought were related to traditional American Indian Philosophy and Thought and that left hemispheric modes of thought were related to American mainstream philosophy and thought.

In 1981 Dr. Ross synchronistically discovered that the Wakinyan Oyate was a cultural linguistic name for the Christ spirit (see pp 130-133 for details). The message on the shield is that the descending bird (Wakinyan Oyate/Christ Spirit) would bring the two different types of thinking together as one. That is why he has dedicated the book to Dawson No Horse (see epilogue for details).

Published by
Wicóni Wasté
Box 480005
Denver, CO 80248
Copyright © 1989
by Allen Ross

First Printing - March 1989
Second Printing - January 1990
Third Printing - November 1990
Fourth Printing - September 1991
Fifth Printing - March 1992
Sixth Printing - December 1992
Seventh Printing - July 1993
Eighth Printing - June 1994
Ninth Printing - April 1995
Tenth Printing - May 1996
Eleventh Printing - February 1997 (revised edition)
Twelfth Printing - July 1997

LIBRARY OF CONGRESS CATALOGING IN PUBLICATION DATA

Ross, Allen
Mitakuye Oyasin
"We are all Related"
Bibliography: p. 211
89-090095

ISBN 0-9621977-0-X

DEDICATED IN MEMORY OF:

DAWSON HAS NO HORSES

Dawson was a husband, father, and grandfather. He announced at powwows, danced traditional dances, and performed Yuwipi ceremonies. Dawson was a Wicasa Wakan (Holy Man) who had lived at Wakpamni lake, South Dakota.

ACKNOWLEDGEMENTS

All Sun Dancers
All Tribal medicine people
All Sweat Lodge Warriors
American Indian Unity Church
Supported in part by the North Dakota Humanities Council
Native American Ministries of the Evangelical Lutheran Church in America
My parents - Harvey and Agnes Ross for their support
My wife - Dorothy Brave Eagle for her kindness, patience, and Love
My Typists -   Achaessa Romero
                Jean Katus
My Illustration Artist - John Beheler
Barbara Vitale for her helpfulness
Richard and Judith Downer

My Children: Dana   My Grandchildren: Krystal Dawn
                Dawn   Santee Kay
                Cindy   Kelsea Lynn
                Sandy   Kaitlyn Leigh
                Hok   Natalie Marie
                Fred   Theodore Allen
                                                 Tyson James

My Hunka Children: Amber No Horse
                      Ralphie Hernandez
                      Kristi Blue Bird
                      Chaske Luger
                      Elgin Head
                      Stanley Natchez
                      Florentine Blue Thunder
                      Joe Marino
                      Sandra Rolshoven

Hunka Brothers: Jody Luger
                      Chuck Lewis
                      Michael Kastner
                      Claude Two Elk

Hunka Sister: Linda Mitchell

PREFACE

Mitakuyapi
"My Relatives"

On August 16, 1987, a group of concerned Native Americans organized a conference during the Harmonic Convergence. Approximately 1000 people attended this three-day conference. I had the opportunity to present my entire lecture series there. Numerous requests were made for written material on my series. Up to that point, I had deliberately kept the information oral/visual because I felt that this method of presenting it was a whole-brain approach to learning. But the conference participants argued that an oral/visual presentation limits the number of people who can benefit from the material. With this in mind, I decided to prepare a manuscript for publication. This book, *Mitakuye Oyasin*, grew out of my need to illustrate how we are all related.

I was born at Pipestone, Minnesota on October 25, 1940 at 1:40 p.m. Pipestone is known as a place of peace among the tribes who went there to mine the red stone for their sacred pipes. I'm a member of the Mdewakantonwan tribe. This tribe is one of the original seven tribes of the Dakota Nation. (The Dakota Nation is more commonly known as the Sioux.) Mdewakantonwan, translated into English, means "spirit water people." I was born of Santee, Sicangu, Ponca, Irish and Scottish blood. My earlier years were spent on the Flandreau, Rosebud, and Pine Ridge Reservations in South Dakota. The people of these reservations were at one time considered part of the Great Dakota Nation. Dakota, interpreted into English, means "Related People." (The Dakota Nation is also known as the Seven Campfires. It contains three linguistic dialects--the Dakota, the Lakota, and the Nakota. Out of respect for the two largest dialects, I have used various designations throughout the text--D/Lakota, Dakota/Lakota, Dakota, and Lakota.)

During the past twenty years, American Indians have experienced a renaissance of their language, culture, and religion. Many tribes have become conscious of their original names which, when translated into English, mean "The People." The fact that we are *all* one people is the wholistic view I wish to present in this book.

Ehanamani Emaciyapi
"My name is Walks Among"
a.k.a. Allen (Chuck) Ross

TABLE OF CONTENTS

ILLUSTRATION ARTIST

John Beheler B.S. Ed.
Yankton Sioux Tribal Member
Employed by United Tribes Technical College
Bismark, N.D.

IYESKA

(Interpreter)

In 1962 I was stationed with the 505th Paratrooper Brigade in Mainz-Gonsenheim, Germany. During my military tour in Europe, I became aware of German clubs that studied American Indians. One day I met a member from one of these clubs. To my surprise, I learned that the German knew more about the history of the D/Lakota people than I did! At first I was ashamed of myself for not knowing my own history. Then I decided to learn all I could about D/Lakota history and culture.

In grade school, I attended a Bureau of Indian Affairs (BIA) boarding school. The Indian children in this school did not have an opportunity to learn their own history. The high school I attended was a Christian missionary boarding school. My early influence was strictly Christian and western civilization. Therefore, beginning to learn D/Lakota history and culture was new to me. At first my interest led me to read many books on the subject. Then I talked to older D/Lakota people about the history and culture as they remembered it. Later I became actively involved in pow-wows (Indian dances) as a dancer, singer, and announcer. Only recently have I become actively involved in the D/Lakota religion.

As a recent participant in my own traditional culture, I have asked myself, "Why do we do certain things or believe certain stories? There must be a reason behind our traditional beliefs." My search for my origins as a Dakota person led me into a fascinating search for the origins of the red man.

Western civilization teaches that the ancestors of the American Indian arrived in the Americas approximately 20,000 years ago via the Bering Straits from northeast Asia. But D/Lakota oral history recorded that the red man has always been in the western hemisphere and in particular, in North America. I pondered this.

1

Authorities in western civilization agree that humans did not evolve in the western hemisphere.

Because of the German Indian Club experience, I wanted to find out about the history and culture of my tribe, so I started a search for my roots. First, I began looking for my identity in books, reading everything I could get my hands on about the history and culture of the D/Lakota people. I studied the books. Later, I returned home and spoke to my grandparents. They proceeded to tell traditional stories, and I asked them, "How come you never told us this before?"

"Well, no one ever asked us," was their reply.

The elders have a wealth of knowledge. Not only my grandparents, but everybody's grandparents have a wealth of knowledge about the era that they lived in. When I started talking with them, visiting with the older folks, I got a little bit different version than what was in the books. Basically it was the same, but still there were differences.

In 1967, I wanted to learn how to do traditional D/Lakota dances. I put together a dance outfit that consisted of a head roach, eagle feather bustle, ankle bells, beaded breach cloth, bone necklace and breastplate, beaded arm band, tufts and moccasins. I was really afraid of being ridiculed. It was very hard for me to start dancing; I had to force myself to participate. When I began, I really danced awkwardly, like a Hollywood Indian. One, two, one, two. That was me; that's the way I was dancing. And maybe I still dance like that today, I don't know. But I felt a need to learn. Later I wanted to learn how to sing traditional D/Lakota songs. I sat around the drums listening to songs, learning the songs.

I went into my first sweat lodge in 1974. I had never been in one before because I had grown up in a Christian missionary home. We went to church every morning and evening, plus three times on Sunday. Later when many of us who went to missionary schools got together and shared experiences, some of the kids who had gone to other mission schools used to tease us. They'd say, "You Bishop Hare School boys have flat knees." Well, they weren't too far from wrong! That was my upbringing, and so, when I went into the sweat lodge, I didn't know what to expect. There are no books on how to go into a sweat lodge. Almost all Indian tribes use one for ceremonial purposes. The D/Lakota sweat lodge is built from a willow frame and is covered with canvas. In the old days, it was covered with buffalo or elk hide. The floor of the Navajo sweat lodge is several feet below the surface of the surrounding earth. The wood frame is covered with earth and sand, and a blanket forms the door flap. The Hoopa Indians of northern California traditionally utilized a sweat house. The floor of their house, like the Navajo, was also lower than the level of the earth. You entered it through a door on the side and left it through a circular opening at the opposite end. Whole groups of people participated in the ceremony at the same time. The Carib Indians of South America use the sweat lodge for medicinal purposes. The Mayan Indians of Guatemala have been discovered to have used sweat rooms inside some of their temples.

When you enter the D/Lakota sweat lodge and close the flap, it's totally dark inside. The door man has placed the hot rocks in the center and the sweat lodge leader has offered the sacred water to the holy rocks, creating steam. I was sitting there, and it started getting hot. Then the participants began to pray. The sweat lodge leader offered more water to the rocks.

Soon it was so darn hot in there I thought to myself, "What in the world am I doing in here? These guys are roasting me alive!" Thinking about why I was there, I suddenly had a realization: "You came in here to pray." So I started praying. The hotter it got, the stronger I prayed. The leader offered more water. In a little while, I was right down next to the ground. And I was really praying! Then I reached a point (it's hard to explain) where I went, "Poof!"--into a different dimension or something like that. At this point all that heat seemed to diminish.

That was my first experience in D/Lakota ceremonialism.

I was living in Denver in 1977 and teaching at the University of Colorado. I taught in the Native American Studies area: Native American Philosophy and Thought, Native American History, and Native American Art. One day during that year my ankles became swollen to a point where I could not walk. At first I was on crutches, then eventually ended up in a wheelchair. My wife, Dorothy Brave Eagle, and I went to a doctor in Denver. His initial diagnosis indicated that he didn't know what was wrong. He decided to put me in the hospital for a thorough examination, which lasted ten days.

The hospital staff tested everything: my blood, my kidneys, my liver, my chest, my heart. They x-rayed me; they even hooked my head up to a machine and checked my brain waves. You name it, they checked me. At the end of the ten days, the doctor came into the room with all his charts, diagrams, and x-rays. He said, "I'm sorry. I can't find anything wrong with you. A lot of people think that modern medicine is a science, but it isn't. It's an art. All we can do is take a look at organs in your body and see if they are functioning properly. If not, we try to repair them, and if we can't repair the organ, we take it out and put a plastic one in."

I said, "Well, what about my condition?"

"In your case," he replied, "we can't find anything wrong. You have what we call a syndrome."

All he could give me were some pain pills. I got back in the wheelchair and my wife pushed me home. After about a month, I got tired of not being able to walk and not knowing what was wrong. I remembered when I was growing up on the reservation that there was a healing ceremony called "yuwipi."

I asked my wife, "Have you ever been to a yuwipi ceremony?"

She said she had, and added, "That's how I grew up."

"Well, do you think they could help me in that ceremony?"

"I don't know why not," she affirmed, "Other people have been helped many times."

"Okay, that's good enough for me!" I responded.

We loaded up the van and took off for South Dakota. When we got there, we went to Wakpamani Lake. A holy man by the name of Dawson No Horse lived there. I went to his place, gave him tobacco, and requested his services. Since then, I've learned that the proper way to request the services of a holy man is to offer him a sacred pipe filled with tobacco.

"First you have to tie some prayer offerings," he told me.

Because I didn't know what they were, he gave me a brief explanation. You cut a one-inch square of red cloth and place tobacco in the center of the square as you say your prayers, he told me. Then you fold up the corners, forming a little pouch, and tie a string around it. You make one hundred of these pouches. We sat up that first night tying up prayer offerings. Great big ones! Big, fat ones! We took them to Dawson. He really smiled and remarked, "These are good offerings."

Next, we went into the ceremony house. The helpers covered up all the windows and the doors with blankets so no light could get in. Then they took a star quilt and wrapped Dawson up with a rope and tied it. He looked like a mummy. (Yuwipi means to tie up.) They laid him on the floor. The singers began to drum and sing sacred songs. It was the first time I had heard these songs. I was used to hearing pow-wow songs, but these songs were different. I could sense they were spiritual songs the way one tells the difference between sacred and secular music. The spirits came in when the singing started. They were flying around. You could see them. They looked like sparks of light. You could hear them, too. They sounded like wings flapping in the dark. I wasn't surprised; nor was I afraid. During the healing part of the ceremony, a spirit came in and stood in front of where I was sitting. He put his hands on my head. I could actually feel his hands on my head.

I wondered, "Who is this?" I thought, "It's Dawson. He crawled out of that blanket. I don't know how he did it, but he's standing here with his hands on my head."

5

Just as this thought came to mind, Dawson started speaking again. He was still wrapped up on the floor. Looking at where he was lying, I saw the sparks of lights flying all around him. They lit up the area so I could see him.

Then I tried to determine, "Well, who is this over here with his hands on my head?"

I had a lot of questions, like where do these spirits come from? And how can they see in the dark? But I knew that it was a healing ceremony. I went ahead and prayed while this spirit had his hands on my head. All of a sudden, there was a flash of light as I was praying. It was like a circle, a ring of light inside my head. It flashed four times. Next, the singers sang the going-home songs. The spirits left. When the helpers turned on the electric lights, Dawson was sitting there unwrapped. The star quilt was folded neatly beside him with the rope on top of it. I looked down at my ankles and they were still swollen. I tried to walk but couldn't.

Now I was really confused! I thought this was a healing ceremony. My wife Dorothy and I went to visit with Dawson. I asked him, "Am I all right?"

"Yeah," he said, "you're all right. It'll take about a month for your body to cleanse itself, but you're all right."

We went back to Denver and about a month later, the "syndrome" disappeared! Was this a coincidence? Or had something else occurred? I was happy. I was able to run again; I could dance again.

Then Dorothy said to me, "Well, now we have to go home for a 'wopila' ceremony. We need to give thanks."

We loaded up the van again, this time with blankets, food, and items which were to be given to Dawson and to people in need. We returned to South Dakota and went to Dawson's ceremony.

The same thing happened again. The helpers wrapped him up and laid him on the floor. They turned out the lights, and the singers started to sing. In the ceremony Dawson is considered an "iyeska" or interpreter. The spirits can communicate with certain people like Dawson, who then interpret the information to the people. The spirits told Dawson to inform me that they had healed me, and now they wanted a favor in return.

The traditional D/Lakota belief is that everything goes in cycles. They call it "Okawige." If you're good to people, that's going to return to you. If you're wicked to people, that'll come back to you. What you give out, you get back.

After hearing about the spirits' request, I considered what favor I could do as my wopila, my thanksgiving. The idea suddenly came to me: "Sun Dance!" I decided to do the Sun Dance as my thanksgiving to the spirits. When I told Dawson of my decision to sun dance, he was very happy, and told me that before I danced, I must prepare myself by going on a vision quest. "How many days do you want to go on the hill?" he asked me.

I told him, "Four days and four nights."

He was silent for a long time and finally said, "It's really hard. Fours days and four nights are really hard. People aren't as strong now as the people in the old days. It's because of the food we eat, the things we drink. You should think about less time."

"Okay, I'll go three days and three nights," I decided. Dawson hesitated again and repeated the same advice.

Reluctantly, I agreed: "Two days and two nights." Growing up on the reservation with the cultural value of bravery, I felt it would be "chicken" to go fewer than four days and four nights. But I also respected Dawson's suggestions.

On the second evening of my vision quest, I had a dream in which I was visited by three spirits. They told me they wanted to communicate with me while I was here on earth. Then they left. I told Dawson about this dream. He looked at me for a long time and then said, "Study it, Chuck. Study it. Don't grab it and run."

I shared Dawson's comments with Dorothy and she observed, "I think he means that you shouldn't believe you're somebody special just because of one dream. You need to wait and think about it." After finishing my vision quest, I now prepared for the Sun Dance.

The Sun Dance is held for four days and four nights. Traditionally, the participants took no food or water during this time. The first day of my Sun Dance experience, the temperature was 102 degrees. My mouth dried up. On the second day my throat began to dry out. My whole mouth and throat were completely dry on the third day. I looked around and the other dancers didn't appear to be suffering that much; I forced myself to keep on dancing. It was very hard, but my pride prodded me into continuing.

That afternoon, weaving back and forth, I was ready to faint from the heat and exhaustion. I thought, "What in the world am I doing out here? I could be home in my air-conditioned apartment drinking ice cold soda pop."

Dawson must have read my mind because he said, "You made a pledge to come out here. Nobody asked you to do this."

Reflecting back on that experience, I knew this was the Indian way. They don't ask you to participate in the ceremonies. The decision must be yours.

That was my first wopila.

After you have participated in the Sun Dance for the four obligatory years and have felt the great honor to dance the Sun Dance on behalf of all the people, then you have a give-away. Having finished my fourth Sun Dance, my wife and I loaded up the van with items and again went back to South Dakota for another give-away.

Later I was talking with a holy man named Norbert Running, and I said, "Well, I've completed my fourth Sun Dance. I'm finished now."

He sat there a long time, looking down, and then he commented, "You know, once you pick up the pipe, you're never finished." (The pipe is used in sacred ceremonies.)

I had a lot of questions about D/Lakota ceremonies but no answers. When I was first in the ceremonies, I felt like raising my hand and saying, "Wait a minute, Mr. Holy Man. Explain to me what's going on here."

In spite of my many questions, I didn't want to go to the ceremonies with a paper and pencil or a tape recorder because I didn't want to be like the people who study Indians on the reservations every summer. I remember when I was a boy, a man from New York came to the reservation. Some friends and I spent a summer pitching hay with him. We used to tease him and make fun of him. We didn't know it, but he was an anthropologist. He was studying us.

He returned to New York and wrote a book on his experiences. And I was in that book. He wrote, "Native Americans have lost their culture. Native Americans have lost their language. Native Americans have lost their religion." That was me he was describing! That's why I didn't want to appear as if I were an outsider studying the ceremonies. We've been studied to death. Too many come to the reservation to study us. I feel these people have what's called "tunnel vision." They see us only one way--their way.

The fact still remained that I had no answers to my questions about the ceremonies.

In 1978 I returned to college to finish my doctorate degree. While registering for classes, there was one time slot I couldn't find a course to fill. Reviewing the catalog, I eventually found one course that was offered at that time. It was called Jungian Psychology. I hated psychology! I'd never heard of Carl Gustav Jung. But I had to take the course because it was all that was offered at that time. I went to class, and the professor began explaining Jung's concept of psychology. I raised my hand and said, "Hey, wait a minute. Do you know what you're talking about? This is traditional D/Lakota philosophy and thought. These things you're talking about are practiced at home. Some of them happen in the ceremonies."

9

I'd like to share the similarities I discovered between Jungian psychology and traditional D/Lakota philosophy and thought.

JUNGIAN PSYCHOLOGY AND BRAIN HEMISPHERICY COMPARED WITH D/LAKOTA THOUGHT

Dr. Jung declared that the mind can be divided into three levels. He didn't call it the mind, he called it the "psyche." He figured that in order for people to appreciate his psychology, he would use big words. The bigger the word, the more difficult it was to understand and the more appreciation people would have.

The top part of the psyche, or the mind, Dr. Jung called the conscious, also known as the ego. This is the active thinking part of the mind, the part you use when you're awake.

Below that area is a level he called the personal unconscious where all the memories since birth are. Dr. Jung said your mind has the ability to remember everything it saw or heard from the moment you were born. All that knowledge is stored in the personal unconscious. This area of the mind is either repressed or suppressed. In other words, we can't remember those early events. Under hypnosis, a person can be put in contact with this area of the mind to help him or her remember experiences from the earliest years. Under hypnosis there are some people who can even remember when they were born!

The lower level of the mind Dr. Jung called the collective unconscious. He felt that latent memory traces from your entire ancestral past are stored in this area. Any time you want knowledge or information, it's within the collective unconscious. A person under hypnosis can make contact with this part of the mind also.

According to Jung, modern man is out of balance. Regardless of race or sex, modern man is conscious-oriented. And modern man neglects the unconscious portions of his mind. Dr. Jung indicated that there are different methods of communicating with or utilizing the lower levels of the mind.

One technique he used was dreams. Dreams, he said, are unconscious completion of conscious content. In other words,

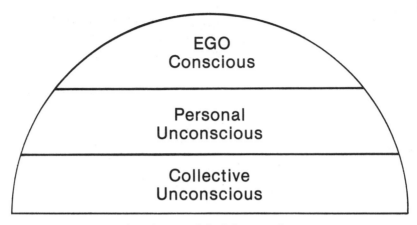

EGO
Conscious

Personal
Unconscious

Collective
Unconscious

Jungian model of the psyche

dreams are coming from the unconscious, penetrating consciousness. And since the unconscious portion of the mind cannot talk, when it penetrates consciousness, it comes in the form of images and symbols, thoughts and ideas. Dr. Jung remarked that modern man needs to understand the language of the unconscious. Example: if you have a dream of a fish coming up and kissing you on the hand, that doesn't mean that tomorrow a fish is going to walk up and grab your hand and kiss it. The fish is a symbol for something. The kissing of the hand is a symbol for something. It's the symbology that we need to understand. Few dreams have a literal interpretation.

In studying D/Lakota history, I found that we had dream societies a hundred years ago. The people used dreams to guide their lives at that time. A person would have the holy man of the dream society interpret the dream in a ceremony. Maybe the dream foretold an event. The people attending the ceremony would then share this information with friends and relatives.

Another way of communicating with the lower levels of the mind is through meditation. There are two types--concentration and mindfulness. In the concentration kind, you concentrate on one image or idea. Maybe your image is a cross, or it may be a medicine wheel. You can use any kind of symbol. You meditate on it until thoughts start coming up which pertain to the image.

The other variety of meditation, mindfulness, is allowing all thoughts to come up into consciousness. When you receive a thought, you recognize it and let it go. The next thought comes up--you recognize it--and then let it go. You just let these thoughts flow. You'll be surprised at what comes into your mind!

When I first came across the word meditation, I had the image of people sitting cross-legged and humming, "Om." Later I found out you don't have to do that to meditate. To meditate in that fashion is okay, but if it doesn't work for you, there are other ways to communicate with the lower levels of the mind.

In researching Native American ceremonialism, I found that the yuwipi ceremony was nothing more than a means or an aid to help the holy men make contact with the other side, or what Jung calls the collective unconscious. Traditional Native American societies did not have a written language. In the traditional culture, any time you wanted knowledge or information, you went to a ceremony. The iyeska made contact with the other side and was able to answer your questions.

Another of Dr. Jung's principles was that there is no such thing as coincidence. When I returned to college and ended up in the Jungian Psychology course which contained many answers to questions I had about Native American ceremonialism, I thought it was coincidence. But I learned that when two things happen at the same time, it is known as synchronicity. Under the law of synchronicity, there is a purpose, a plan, a reason for everything that happens. To be more precise, the Jungian definition of synchronicity is described in *Theories of Personality* by Calvin S. Hall and Gardner Lindzey:

13

Synchronistic phenomena are attributed to the nature of archetypes. An archetype is said to be *psychoid* in character; that is, it is both psychological and physical. Consequently, an archetype can bring into consciousness a mental image of a physical event even though there is no direct perception of the physical event. The archetype does not cause both events; rather it possesses a quality that permits synchronicity to occur.

Upon returning to South Dakota, I mentioned this law of synchronicity to Dawson, explaining to him what it meant. To my surprise, he exclaimed, "Do! [pronounced "doe"] That's right. You were guided to be in that class so you could learn about these things and then be able to share them with the people." It was with Dawson's support that I studied Jungian Psychology.

Dr. Jung has written some twenty volumes. I found his information very difficult to understand, his psychology hard to digest. I continued to study, though, because of my interest.

Delving into psychology, I was gradually led into studies about the brain. I knew that the brain had two hemispheres, but I did not realize that each side of the brain was dominant in different modes of thinking. The first information on brain hemisphericy was released by Dr. Roger Sperry. He won a Nobel Prize for medicine for his work. He studied individuals who were known as split-brained patients. These people had their corpus callosum (a cord that connects the two hemispheres of the brain) severed for medical reasons. Dr. Sperry discovered, in his work with these patients, hemispheric dominance for different thinking modes. Poring over his research, once again I could see, as in Jungian psychology, how it related to traditional Native American philosophy and thought. I want to share the observations that became evident to me.

The left side of the brain controls logic, linearity, reading and writing, time orientation, and masculine expression. The right side of the brain is dominant in instinct, wholism, dance, art, spatiality, and feminine expression.

The left side of the brain is dominant in analytical thinking and reasoning. Another characteristic of the left side of the brain is linear thinking, where the brain can see only parts of the whole. It sees the parts, analytically adding them up, eventually arriving at the whole. Some people have expressed linear thinking as straight- line thinking, A to Z, 1 to 100, beginning to end. The left side of the brain is what we use for reading and writing.

The left side is also time-oriented. Left-brain-dominant people constantly worry about the time. I think Germany is the most left-brained country I ever visited. Clocks hang everywhere, and the Germans really pride themselves with being on time.

Brain hemispheric research has concluded that the majority of our society emphasizes the functions of the left side of the brain. Consequently, we live in a left-brain world. Reading this, I questioned how we ended up in such an out-of-balance society. Research explained that the culprit was the educational systems. Our educational systems over-emphasize the functions of the left side of the brain.

An example is reading and writing. We go to school, we learn how to write words, we put the words into sentences, we put the sentences together into paragraphs, then combine the paragraphs into term papers. Education stresses that if we want any knowledge or information, we must learn how to do library research. Consequently, we're book people. We have reached a point where educators say that if knowledge or information is not in a book, we shouldn't believe it. It has to be written down, it has to be somebody's research to be credible.

The research on brain hemphericy is pointing the finger at educators. We are the culprits--the guilty ones. I'm an educator and when the researchers started pointing the finger at me, I got very sensitive about that. I wanted to understand the functions of the brain that we do not emphasize in education, those related to the right hemisphere.

Instinct is one of the functions of the right side of the brain. When a person gets a feeling about something, he or she must learn to accept it as valid. This acceptance is what we need to start teaching our children so they can learn to use their instinctive information. Another right-hemispheric function is wholistic thinking where one is able to see the big picture in a single glance. Then one works back to the pieces, the reverse of linear thinking.

Wholistic thinking is what is used in traditional ceremonies. An example is the pipe ceremony. The tobacco placed in the pipe represents the green things, the four-leggeds, the winged ones, and all the things in the water. You ask all these things to come into the pipe. You offer the pipe to the four directions, up to the mystery spirits of the universe, and down to Mother Earth. When you smoke the pipe, you're asking all these things to come into you and to be one with you. That's wholistic thinking. That's a right-hemispheric approach to religion. In the D/Lakota language, when we finish our prayers, we say, "Mitakuye Oyasin," which is interpreted literally as "all my relatives." It means that we are all related. To me, that's right- brain thinking.

Additional functions of the right hemisphere are dance, art, and music. In traditional ceremonies we dance our prayers, we sing our prayers, and we use four sacred colors.

The right side of the brain is spatial in its time orientation. That means that the right hemisphere is not as interested in "clock" time as the left side, which is concerned with preciseness. An example: Work is generally scheduled according to the clock. Modern religion is scheduled according to the calendar. Native Americans use a concept called "Indian time." You do something whenever it feels right. That's my understanding of spatial time orientation.

The left side of the brain is masculine in one of its expressions, and the right side is feminine. I have a daughter in college named Dawn who believes in ERA and women's liberation. When she learned about brain hemisphericy, she said, "Now I understand

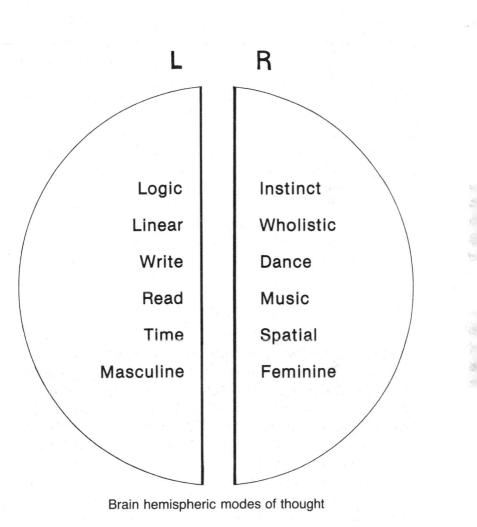

Brain hemispheric modes of thought

why there's so much male chauvinism. It's because we live in a left-brain dominant world!"

One day a student in my Traditional Native American Philosophy and Thought class at the University of Colorado came to me and said, "Did you know that the material you're teaching us in this class is being taught in another class I'm taking? But that class isn't called Native American Philosophy and Thought."

I asked her the name of the course, and she answered, "It's called Parapsychology." That immediately grabbed my interest. What is it that could be the same as traditional Native American philosophy and thought? I wanted to learn more, but I wanted to approach it with an open mind.

I can remember when I was growing up that there were always people coming to the reservation trying to save us, but they did not have an open mind. As I mentioned before, I felt they had tunnel vision. I didn't want to have this view. That's why I said to myself, "I'm going to go to this class and make up my own mind whether to believe the parapsychological teachings." I sat in the teacher's class, and she began to explain the story of creation. Listening to her explanation, I became very excited. My hand shot into the air. I told her, "What you have just explained is identical to the D/Lakota creation story." I'd like to share this comparison.

In the teacher's explanation of creation, she said that a mass of energy started from the center of the universe and expanded, dividing into individual portions of energy. The number of these individual energies is so immense it cannot be counted. This tremendous amount of energy is separate, yet it is only one. Next, the teacher said that when a body is born, one of those energies comes in to give the body life. You live your life, and then you reach a point where the body dies. She commented that if you live your life in balance and harmony with everything, (what is known as the Red Road in D/Lakota philosophy), then when the body dies, the energy is released and goes back to the center of the universe where it came from. But, she asserted, if you live

18

your life for the self only, (what is known as the Black Road in D/Lakota philosophy,) when the body dies, the energy is released, comes back, and is reborn into a new body. This process is known as "kini" in D/Lakota philosophy.

The D/Lakota story that coincides with this parapsychological creation story says when a person dies, his or her spirit goes up to the Milky Way and then south. At the south end, there's a fork in the Milky Way. Reaching this fork, the spirit is greeted by a woman. This old woman says, "What did you do on earth? Did you live for yourself--greedy, materialistic, selfish? Or did you live in balance and harmony with all things?" If you are judged as living a selfish life, or you've lived on the Black Road, the old woman pushes you off the Milky Way and you come back to earth. You're born into a new body and given another chance to grow and expand. Or if it's determined that you've lived in balance and harmony, that you've lived on the Red Road, then you're allowed to continue on the Milky Way--back to the center of the universe.

Up to this point, all that I have shared and what I will continue to share are personal experiences. I'm not asking anybody to believe them. I'll simply share them and we'll just let them be.

I would like to expand upon the Red Road philosophy. It was about ten years ago that I first came in contact with it. At that time, I was drinking alcohol very regularly. I'd drunk for 22 years. I was an alcoholic. But I didn't believe I was an alcoholic; I thought I was a social drinker. Then one day one of my principals, Milo Buffalo approached me and remarked, "Chuck, I don't know whether you realize this or not, but you're a leader in this community. The community looks to you for leadership. Maybe you should watch your drinking." I never realized I was drinking too much. When Milo pointed this out to me, I got to thinking about it.

One Monday when I returned to work after a three-day drunk, I told myself, "I'd better do something about my drinking." I decided to go on the wagon. This lasted about three weeks. Then

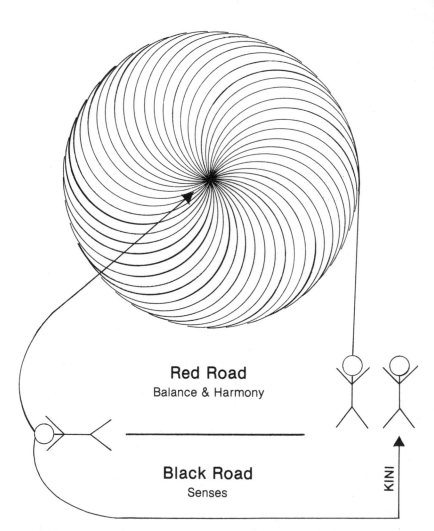

Red Road
Balance & Harmony

Black Road
Senses

KINI

This diagram illustrates the evolutionary growth of the soul

on Friday afternoon at 4:30, something started pulling on me. The temptation tugged at me, and I said to myself, "No! I'm not going to drink. I'm on the wagon." The more I said "no" to drinking, the stronger the temptation became. Eventually, I broke down. I phoned my first wife, Pat. I lied to her. I made an excuse about having to attend a meeting. Then I sneaked out, went downtown, and got drunk. I went to the bars and called out, "Set 'em up! If the superintendent drinks, everybody drinks."

The following Monday morning I returned to work. Not only did I have a hangover and an upset stomach, but I also felt guilty. You know, in this left-brain world when you make a mistake, you're taught to feel guilty about it. So I got back on the wagon. Then three weeks later, temptation came again. And once again I broke down, repeating the same scenario. Back and forth, back and forth. That's when I realized I couldn't stay sober by myself.

I went to Alcoholics Anonymous. I didn't feel quite right, though, because most of the ones who went were older than I and were mostly hardcore cases. And besides that, there were no Indians in AA. I was the only one. Because I really wanted to try, I visited with the AA people, and they assigned me a person to call when I got into trouble. When temptation came again, I called the number--but there was no answer. I went out and got drunk. Alcoholics Anonymous didn't work for me.

Next I started a program with antabuse. Antabuse is a little white tablet that you take and if you ever drink with it in your system, you get very, very sick. The idea is that it's kind of like a crutch to help you. On antabuse, I went to the clinic every Monday and the nurse gave me a tablet and a glass of water. The doctor wrote something down on his pad. I thought to myself, "Who are these two people giving me this antabuse? I'm smarter than they are!" I'd hide the tablet under my tongue and when I went out the door, I'd spit it out. Then I'd go downtown and get drunk. That system didn't work for me either.

21

Eventually, Pat and I ended up in a divorce. Then I realized I was really in trouble with my drinking. It was about this time I had become interested in Native American ceremonialism. I went to a holy man and asked him for help. He told me to get on the Red Road. "Pray to Wakan Tanka (Great Spirit) to help you walk the Red Road." I started praying to get on the Red Road, but I did not understand it. One night when I went to sleep, curious about this Red Road, I had a dream. A red road was in the dream, floating in the air. It was floating in the middle of my dream. And I was walking on it. Some friends who were sober were on the left side of the road, and they were calling me to come join them. I said, "No!"

When I said no, there appeared, on the right side of the road, a group of my friends who were honky-tonking, really boozing it up. They called to me, "Come over and join us." I said, "No! I want to stay in the middle. I want to continue walking this red road." When I awoke the next morning, I quickly wrote down my dream.

This is what has helped me with my sobriety. When temptation comes, I don't say, "Yes," and I don't say, "No." I say, "Later." I just keep walking the Red Road--down the middle. When you're in the middle, you don't go to either extreme. You allow both sides to exist.

I recognized that this concept was wholistic thinking, a right-hemispheric way of thinking. In the beginning, I did not understand. I'm a book person. I went to school, I learned how to read and write, I learned how to do library research. I learned how to write term papers, a thesis, and a dissertation. I have a doctorate degree in education, but I could not do this right-brain mode of thought activity called walking the Red Road. I had to pray for it every day.

Later when I studied Jungian psychology, I discovered Jung espoused a similar philosophy. He called it transcendent function. Where did he get these ideas and why were they the same

22

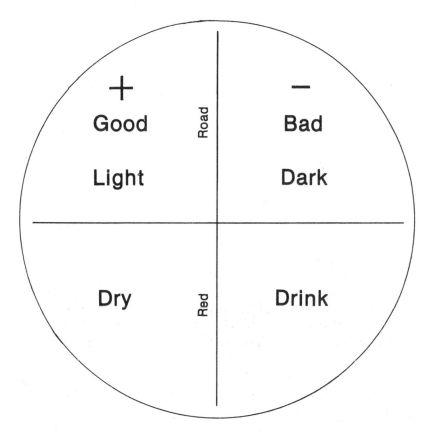

The Red Road concept is the same as the Alcohol Anonymous philosophy "One day at a time".

as ours? Dr. Jung claimed that to attain transcendent function, one needs to maintain a balance between pairs of opposites, between feeling and thinking, between sensation and intuition. He stated that the way to maintain this balance is to become aware of the mood that you're in at all times. That's harder than a person realizes! Maybe you laugh too loudly, for instance, but you're not aware of it, and it turns people off. Or maybe you're scratching somewhere, a place where you're not supposed to be scratching in public. Everybody sees it except you. Being able to see behind you without looking is an extreme example of transcendent function.

The Jungian idea of balance, coupled with the Red Road philosophy, is what helped me achieve sobriety. I have practiced this successfully for fourteen years.

I learned more about the Red Road through my participation in the Sun Dance. The Sun Dance circle is outlined by the four sacred directions, the circle representing the entire universe. At the center of the circle is a sacred tree which has two dominant branches on top, which stand for the duality of everything in the universe. Everything in the universe is in pairs of opposites: positive/negative; good/bad. This is one of the teachings of D/Lakota ceremonialism. The sacred tree is Wakan Tanka (God), and it's at the center of the Sun Dance circle (universe).

Dr. Jung also declared that everything within the psyche is in pairs of opposites. This thinking is identical to the philosophy taught in parapsychology, that the creative energy came from the center of the universe. Modern physics has shown that everything in the universe is either positive or negative. How did the Indians get this knowledge?

A principle of Native American ceremonialism is that we do not proselytize. We do not go out and knock on doors. If a person participates in the ceremonies, that is his decision. If a person participates in a Sun Dance, that is his pledge. I recognized some truth to this philosophy. If you knock on doors, proselytizing reli gion, then you assume you are better than others and you get yourself out of balance.

In Jungian psychology, it is taught that if you're out of balance, either too far to the good or too far to the bad, the shadow will penetrate consciousness and control you. The shadow is the negative side of the personality, equated with the Christian concept of the devil.

Have you seen the movie "Elmer Gantry"? It's a prime example of a person being out of balance, with the shadow penetrating consciousness. Gantry kept oscillating back and forth between good and bad. He didn't understand the Red Road, the balance.

From my personal experience, I have found it hard to walk the Red Road. I had to teach myself when temptation came--not to say "no" and not to say "yes," but to say "later" and just keep on walking the Red Road.

ORIGINAL TEACHINGS OF THE RED MAN

One of the original teachings of the D/Lakota is that you live your life here on earth in a certain way, either according to the Red Road or according to the Black Road. If you lived on the Red Road, your spirit returns to the center of the universe when the body dies. If, on the other hand, you lived on the Black Road during your life, your spirit, when the body dies, would be released and returned to earth to be reborn in a new body. This we call "kini."

Other tribal groups also held beliefs about reincarnation, the Winnebago, for example. One of their original teachings involved their medicine society, which professed a complicated theology based on reincarnation.

In the Hopi view, the universe was divided into two parts, the upper or people world and the lower or spirit world. The Hopi believe a person lives his life and when the body dies, the spirit journeys to the spirit world and is reborn.

Original teachings of the Eskimos, the Aleuts and the Tlingits, all base their religious beliefs on reincarnation.

Originally, most Indians believed that one may be born again and again. Some claim to have knowledge of a former life. This is one of our original teachings--a belief in the evolution of one's spirit through numerous lifetimes.

Sigmund Freud, the father of modern psychology, believed that one was born with a pre-determined base of information. He called this the "id." Carl Jung also believed that a person was born with a pre-set base of knowledge, which he termed the collective unconscious. I didn't know at this time whether Freud and Jung believed in reincarnation, but I couldn't help wondering how they would have explained the knowledge within the collective unconscious that pertained to previous lives.

Dr. Jung stated that the mind or the psyche can be divided into two parts: the conscious and the unconscious. The conscious portion of the mind is also known as the ego. Within the unconscious were two parts that Jung named the personal and the collective. It is the collective unconscious portion of the mind that Dr. Jung felt contained latent memory traces from one's entire ancestral past.

Dr. Jung said that the stages of life for each individual are: infancy, early childhood, middle age, and old age. He remarked that when a person is born, all that exists is the collective unconscious. From that moment on, the consciousness starts to develop. It continues to develop until early childhood when at puberty, the conscious breaks free from the unconscious. The conscious mind becomes dominant through middle age. Upon reaching old age, consciousness starts to revert back into the unconscious. At death, the conscious then be comes part of the collective unconscious. I considered this and wondered, "Is this the reason that when a person reaches an extreme elderly age, he begins acting like a child again?"

Traditional D/Lakota philosophy taught that a father would not pick up a newborn until the newborn developed a personality of his own. It was felt that the newborns were still in contact with the spirit world until they developed their own personality.

Dr. Jung commented that the conscious part of the mind is the mind of western man, and the unconscious part of the mind is the mind of eastern man. Thomas Blakeslee, in his research on brain hemisphericy, equated the conscious mind with the left side of the brain, and the unconscious with the right side. (I personally have difficulty accepting Blakeslee's interpretation because of my training indicating that the brain and the psyche serve separate purposes.)

Universal thought forms known as archetypes are found within the unconscious mind. Archetype means "first type." Dr. Jung said the most common archetypes existing within the collective unconscious of each individual are: birth, rebirth, death, power, magic, unity, hero, child, supreme being, shadow, wise old man, earth mother, animal, animus, and anima. I'd like to take a closer look at three of these archetypes--the hero, the shadow, and the supreme being.

According to Dr. Jung, the archetypes have cultural names. The supreme being archetype is known to the Christians as God, to the Moslems as Allah and to the D/Lakota people as Tunkasila/Wakan Tanka. The archetype of the shadow is known to the Christians as the devil, to the Moslems as Iblis, and to the D/Lakota people as Wakan Sica. Christians know the hero archetype as Jesus, the Moslems as Mohammed, and the D/Lakota people as Ta Tanka Ska Win.

Upon evaluating this information, I couldn't help but notice the hero archetype for the book religions was a male, while that same archetype for the D/Lakota people was a woman--the White Buffalo Calf Woman. For the Navajo, it was Changing Woman; for the Hopi, Corn Woman; and for the Taos people, Deer Mother. It made me remember the research on brain hemisphericy. The left side of the brain is dominant in masculine expression, and the right side is dominant in feminine expression. Is this the reason why the D/Lakota people have a female for their hero archetype? I don't know.

I wanted to compare Jungian psychology with traditional D/Lakota philosophy and thought. What Jung called the conscious mind or the ego, D/Lakota people would call the senses. Native Americans would call the unconscious portion of the mind the spirit level.

Dr. Jung reported that the archetypes penetrate consciousness through dreams, visions, instinct, and symbology. He found dreams to be a method of communicating with the unconscious mind, and, further more, they are unconscious completion of conscious content. He also said that when dreams are analyzed properly, they can be used as a means to guide a person's life.

My studies in D/Lakota history pointed to a similar concept. Two hundred years ago we had dream societies with such names as the Buffalo, Elk, Bear, Wolf, Thunder, and Winkte Societies. It was determined which society a person belonged to by the type of dream he had. Example: if he dreamed of an elk, he belonged to that society.

One day in discussing the names of these dream societies with a Catholic priest who was an expert on the Lakota language (In fact, he published a dictionary on the Lakota language.), I mentioned the society name "Winkte." I could see a blank in his face. He sounded out the word and said, "To kill the woman," adding, "What kind of society was this?" It dawned on me that even though he was an expert in the language, he knew nothing of the culture. I explained to him what the Winkte Society was all about.

I am grateful to the priest for giving me a greater understanding of the winkte. When he said winkte meant to kill the woman, my thoughts returned to my Jungian psychological studies. Dr. Jung said that within each of us, there is an opposite. Within each man there is a female, the archetype of the anima. Each woman has a male within her, the archetype of the animus. When these archetypes penetrate consciousness, Dr. Jung related, you are no longer you; you become that archetype. In traditional times, the winkte was known as being a special person, and some people even felt they were "wakan" (holy). Jungian psychology, then, gave me the understanding I needed to fully comprehend what was happening to an individual known as winkte. I reasoned, "Was the winkte called special or wakan because that individual had the ability to communicate with the unconscious mind?"

The Jungian concept of reverse psychology also helped me to understand more about the winkte. A question arose: In order to kill the woman within the male, would one need to allow her to exist? I know that in the traditional societies, the winkte took pride in doing such female activities as beading, quilting, leatherwork.

People have commented to me that in today's society there are more and more homosexuals. Why? Another thought occurred to me: "Is it because the dominant society keeps suppressing the homosexual, resulting in anima archetypes penetrating consciousness?"

Another method of communicating with the unconscious portion of the mind is that of meditation. I have learned of two types of meditation in my studies: concentration and mindfulness. In the first type, a person concentrates on a single thought or a single image until an answer penetrates consciousness. In the second type, a person allows an image or a thought to penetrate consciousness. He thinks on each thought and then releases it. Using this method, a person gets a variety of messages that need to be logically organized later. Traditional D/Lakota people used both of these types when they went on a vision quest.

Yet another technique used by traditional D/Lakota individuals to communicate with the collective unconscious or what we call the spirit level is that of the sacred pipe. When one uses the sacred pipe, the tobacco that is placed in the bowl represents all living things: the winged ones, the green things, the four-leggeds, and all the things in the water. After the tobacco is put in the pipe, the pipe is offered to the four sacred directions. I asked myself why. (I feel that I am a left-brain man and I continually want to know why.) Why four directions, why not eight, why not twelve, why not thirteen, why four? Then I read in *Your Electro-Vibratory Body* by Victor Beasley a statement that all matter has four poles.

When a person uses the pipe, the smoke represents the spirits of all things that were placed in the pipe. The individual asks to become one with the earth and all things on it. Is this the reason for offering the pipe to the four sacred directions? Traditionally, the best time to use the sacred pipe was at sunrise and sunset. Once again, I asked myself why.

I remembered when I was in the military service, I took a course on radar training. We were told that the earth's atmosphere is more conducive to the transmission of radio waves at sunrise and sunset. What does the transmission of radio waves at sunrise and sunset have to do with a person saying his prayers at these two times of the day?

Beasley also presented information on brain waves. I found that brain waves were lower frequency radio waves measured in hertz. There are four types: beta, which is 14 to 30 hertz; alpha, which is 8 to 13 hertz; theta, which is 4 to 7 hertz; and delta, which is 1 to 3-1/2 hertz. Any time you have a thought, you're sending radio waves (thought patterns) out into the atmosphere. Is this the reason that traditional people felt that the best time to pray was at sunrise and sunset?

I also became aware that when a person inhales carbon dioxide or smoke, the result is a depression of the conscious mind, thus enabling the individual to make contact with the unconscious mind. Is this the reason the traditional people smoke their pipes in a sacred manner? I know Grandpa told me that to smoke is wakan (holy). The smoke you inhale represents the spirits of everything you put into the pipe. When you breathe in the smoke, you are asking to become one with everything or to become whole.

Dr. Jung stated that religious symbols were originally symbols of wholeness, symbols of the psyche, symbols of balance. In the religious symbol of Taoism, for example, you can see the balance in the patterns of the black and white designs within the circle, known as the yin and the yang. Then, within each design, there is a spot of the opposite. Dr. Jung referred to this symbol as one of balance, the balance between the conscious and the unconscious.

The religious symbol of Hinduism is known as a mandala. Dr. Jung said that the mandala is a symbol of wholeness, of balance. When I looked at the mandala, I noticed that it had four dominant directions within the pattern. Immediately, I recognized it as the four directions symbol that we use in D/Lakota ceremonialism, known as the medicine wheel. I conjectured, "Could the medicine wheel be considered a symbol of balance, a symbol of wholeness, a symbol of the psyche as Dr. Jung taught?"

31

The original symbol of Christianity, Dr. Jung said, was a circle with an "X" within. The lower arm of the "X" was extended later, producing a cross, resulting in the symbol portraying an imbalance. Jung further stated that the symbol now represents man's placing himself above nature and his belief in the delusion that he is superior to nature. Dr. Jung declared that modern man, in this predominantly Christian society, is out of balance.

The symbol of wholeness, represented by the medicine wheel, is still being used in D/Lakota ceremonies today. The center where the "X" crosses is considered the home of Tunkasila, Wakan Tanka, God. I speculated, "If this is the symbol of wholeness, the symbol of the psyche, with Wakan Tanka at the center, then Wakan Tanka or God would be within you."

The next symbol I examined was that of Buddhism. I observed that it was a circle with designs representing balance. In studying this symbol, I was reminded of one of the teachings of Buddhism. The Zen masters have said that if you see Buddha on the road, you should kill him, for he is a false buddha. The Buddha is within you, they teach. Simultaneously, a similar Biblical teaching came to mind, that the kingdom of God is within you.

Dr. Jung has stated that the spiritual problem of modern man is that we're living for the conscious portion of the mind only. We have neglected the unconscious. He said that we are looking outside for salvation when we should be looking inside. This sole looking outward is identical to the D/Lakota teaching of walking the Black Road or living for the senses only.

About seven years ago I gave a presentation at the Community College of Denver. Afterwards, one of the professors came to me and said, "You know the slide that showed how modern man is out of balance, living for the conscious only? It really makes a lot of sense to me. The church I belong to here in Denver--we pride our selves on the fact that we have the largest sound system of any church in the United States."

Jung asserted that regardless of race or sex, modern man is out of balance. We are living for the ego, for the senses. He specified a way to achieve balance as transcendent function, accomplished by becoming aware of the mood you're in at all times. He said that this will place you in the center, between thinking and feeling, between sensation and intuition. Once you have achieved balance, then things from the unconscious will become conscious, and you will become whole.

In the Orient, remarked Fritjof Capra in *The Tao of Physics*, "a virtuous person is...not one who undertakes the impossible task of striving for the good and eliminating the bad, but rather one who is able to maintain a dynamic balance between good and bad." To me that sounds identical to the Red Road philosophy. When you're on the Black Road, you're out of balance. When you're out of balance, the shadow will penetrate consciousness and control you.

Let me give you an example of being spiritually out of balance. Once I applied for a teaching position at Highlands University in Las Vegas, New Mexico. When I went for an interview, I was given a tour of the college, the town, and the mountains behind the college. A huge monastery lay a few miles behind the college in the mountains. I asked, "What is that place?" and was told, "It's an alcoholic rehabilitation center for Catholic priests." I wondered if the priests had somehow gotten out of balance and the shadow had penetrated consciousness, resulting in their alcoholism.

Another example is when I lived in Denver, I used to travel back to South Dakota for the Sun Dance. Not only me, but several others from Denver. I noticed a change in the personality of one of the individuals after every Sun Dance. Each year when he returned from the Sun Dance, everything around him had to be traditional. Soon, you had a difficult time talking to him because everything he talked about was sacred and holy. He was so far out of balance that one day he started drinking. First he lost his job. Then he lost his family. The last time I saw him, he was drunk, and he came up to me and said, "Chuck, you gotta help me. Can you put me up on the hill? [go for a vision quest] I've gotta get straight."

He didn't fully realize that this is what had gotten him out of balance to begin with. The more he went in the direction of being sacred and holy, the more his mind took him in the other direction. The harder he tried to be good, the worse he became because of it. Such a situation is touchy, and it's very difficult to help people who have reached such a point.

As I searched for answers, I came across traditional Native American methods from different tribal groups for attaining spiritual balance. I found that when the Hopi "kachinas" came out to pray, the "koshari" (sacred clowns) appeared. The sacred clowns do everything wrong on purpose. They do everything backwards. They keep the crowd amused with laughter. There are two sides to this ceremony: one is the kachina side, doing things properly; the other the koshari. There is a system of balance within the entire ceremony.

The Navajo have a ceremony called "yebechei." The yebechei are the masked dancers. When they come out, "toneinili," the sacred fools or sacred clowns also appear, doing everything wrong on purpose. Once again, the ceremony has two sides, a balance.

D/Lakota people have a being called "heyoka." The heyoka does everything backwards on purpose. He does everything wrong. But the heyoka is also "wicasa wakan," a holy man with the powers to heal. He is both. He is in balance. He is whole.

Balance is implicit in the Red Road. When you're on the Red Road, you are in the center. Yet, you do not go to either extreme, and you allow both sides to exist. This is accomplished by continually postponing surrendering to temptation, whatever it may be. It is saying "later" instead of "no."

I've always heard that when the medicine men used the sacred pipe, they could communicate with the plants and animals. I wondered if this was possible. A study recorded in Erich Von

Daniken's book *In Search of Ancient Gods* offered an answer. The study was done by Dr. Cleve Backster, a polygraph expert from New York City. One of the things a polygraph measures, he said, was electromagnetic energy.

He performed an experiment with a plant. He attached his polygraph to a plant and then he thought he would light a fire under one of the leaves to see if he could get a reaction on his polygraph. The moment he thought of burning that plant, his polygraph registered a response. The plant heard his thoughts! Now there are books telling us we should talk to our plants, sing to our plants, and that the plants will receive benefits from this type of treatment.

The technique that photographs this energy that all living things give off is termed Kirlian photography. Parapsychologist Dr. Stanley Krippner stated that all living things give off energy-- an aura--which can be photographed. He said that at times this aura is visible. He felt that the aura which Jesus gave off was visible as white light and is recognized in the Bible as a halo. Many religions on earth pictured their holy people with a halo. Tibetan artists, and Buddhists also depicted their holy people with halos.

Another way of communicating with the unconscious mind or with the spirit level is known in D/Lakota as "hanbleceya," which means "to cry for a vision." An individual goes to the top of a high place-- usually the top of a butte or a place in the mountains-- where he fasts for a period of up to four days and four nights, with total abstinence from food and water.

I speculated about a possible connection between the vision quest and the existence of negative ions. In researching the matter, I found that in high places--in particular in the mountains around coniferous trees--there is a large distribution of negative ions. Negative ions are charged particles in the air, and it was discovered that when you breathe negative ions, you are aided in making contact with the collective unconscious portion of the mind. In *Your Electro-Vibratory Body*, Beasley pointed out an experiment with an Indian swami in which the swami breathed pure

Topographic distribution of negative ions.

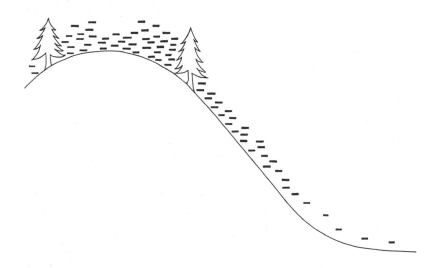

negative ions, resulting in his making contact with the collective unconscious almost instantly.

Later, I discovered that negative ions exist in clouds, particularly around thunder and lightning bolts. I recalled the elders saying that you should not go out for a vision quest until after the "wakinyan" (the thunderstorms) have returned in the spring.

Another method of making contact with the collective unconscious portion of the mind is the sweat lodge ceremony. In this ceremony, as mentioned earlier, rocks are heated to red-hot and are placed in the center of the sweat lodge circle. A person enters with his clothing removed and the sacred water is brought in. The sweat lodge is closed up so that it is totally dark inside. The leader then offers the sacred water to the holy rocks, creating steam. As the steam fills the sweat lodge, each person takes his turn in prayer.

I learned that steam, as well as clouds, contains negative ions. Once again, I could see how breathing it could help a person make contact with the collective unconscious.

Once I was visiting with a German doctor named Alfred Obis. He told me that steam on the body creates an increase in blood circulation. This increase then activates the functions of the body organs to the point where they eliminate toxins in the form of perspiration. He also stated that the increase in blood circulation heightens brain activity and that it was an excellent way of being able to communicate with the unconscious portion of the mind.

Utilizing the persona is yet another example of a procedure for communicating with the unconscious portion of the mind. The persona is a mask which enables the collective psyche to speak. Traditionally, many tribes used sacred masks to communicate with the other side. The Onondaga, for instance, used harvest masks to help make the harvest a success. The Hopi tribe of Arizona has masked dancers which they call kachina. Kachina, translated into English, means "respect for the spirit." When you put on the mask, no longer are you you, rather you are that spirit. It becomes your persona.

The D/Lakota traditional eagle-feather headdress was used as a persona. You earned each feather individually. After you earned twenty-eight feathers, you were entitled to wear the eagle-feather bonnet. These feathers could be acquired by being a good hunter or a good trapper, being a good husband and father, being kind, generous, spiritual (participating in the ceremonies), or being brave in battle. (It was more honorable to touch your enemy than to kill him.) All these qualities went into the persona of the individual when he wore this bonnet. I think Hollywood has distorted the use of the eagle- feather headdress so that it is now most often seen strictly as a "war bonnet."

Many tribes use running as a means of communicating with the other side. Taos Pueblo has a religious race which is very close to the fall equinox. The Hopi tribe, as well as other pueblos, has religious races. The Tarahumara Indians of Mexico are noted world- wide for their running abilities. A book called *Beyond Jogging: The Inner Spaces of Jogging* by Michael Spino talks about running long distances as an aid to reach the inner self.

The Sun Dance, too, assists participants in communicating with the other side or the unconscious mind. During the Sun Dance, you fast for four days and four nights with no food and no water, dancing each day from sunrise to sunset. Traditionally, the Sun Dance was held on the first full moon after the longest day, which usually comes in late June or early July. I questioned, "Why then? Why not in September? Why not in May?"

Investigating this ceremony, I came to find out that all things have movement, all things have vibration. All things contain atoms which have electrons and protons circling the nucleus. I discovered that when two things vibrate in unison, this is known as resonance. When resonance occurs between two objects, there is a maximum exchange of energy.

A resonance occurs between the sun and the earth four times during the year: June 21, September 22, December 22, and March 21. These are the longest day, the shortest day, and the spring and fall equinoxes. Many Native American ceremonies are held at these times. December 22 is when the kachinas come out, when the yebecheis come out. The religious races and sweat lodge ceremonies are held on March 22. June 21 is when the kachina dances which end the summer cycle are held. Right after that is when the D/Lakota have the Sun Dance. More religious races, harvest festivals, and sweat lodge cere monies take place on September 22. How did the ancient Indians know that these times were perfect for communicating with the other side?

At the Sun Dance, each individual has made a pledge to dance for the people. The first time I went to a Sun Dance, I was standing there watching these boys giving their flesh and blood to Wakan Tanka. They did this in a sacred manner by having a peg placed through their skin, a rope tied to this peg, and the other end of the rope tied to the sacred tree in the center. As I watched, I happened to look all the way around the shaded area that surrounds the Sun Dance circle. I noticed that the people were praying; the people were crying. They were sending their thoughts, their pity, their concern to these boys who were suffering for them. I could feel an immense amount of energy in the air within the Sun Dance circle.

Many diseases are cured at the Sun Dance: cancer and diabetes, for example. One of the healing modes used is the laying on of hands where the Sun Dancers pray for the sick by placing their hands on the top of that individual's head. I was curious to know if the radio wave energy produced by the brain could be transmitted through the hands. In seeking an answer, I found a study in Beasley's *Your Electro-Vibratory Body* by Sister Justice Smith of Rosary Hills College in Buffalo, New York who discovered that there was, indeed, a flow of energy between the healer's hands. A related book, *The Kirlian Aura* by Stanley Krippner and Daniel Rubin, described what Kirlian photography can do. A picture was taken of a healer's finger at rest, revealing hardly any energy being emitted at all. A second picture of the healer's finger was taken during the healing process, and it was shown that there was a great deal of electromagnetic energy being emitted from the finger. The reports brought back memories of my Biblical teachings--that the Master healed many individuals by the laying on of hands.

During the Sun Dance, I saw the holy man put his forehead on the back of the dancers when he prayed. I had studied vibratory centers of the body and I wondered if he was activating such a center. The Hopi believe each person has five vibratory centers: the solar plexus, the heart, the throat, the forehead, and the crown. They also believe that as long the spot on top of the head is soft, the spirit can go in and out. After the soft spot hardens, the spirit is locked in the body until death.

The Hindus in India believe the body contains seven vibratory centers called chakras. Where did they get this idea, and why is it so much like the Hopi belief? Every center is activated by a different vibration of light, each of which corresponds to the seven colors of the rainbow. The lowest chakra is activated by the color vibration red. Succeeding chakras on up to the crown are brought into activity by the colors orange, yellow, green, blue, indigo, violet.

When a chakra is activated or opened, it produces a response within the individual. Red produces physical; orange, social; yellow, intellectual; green, self-assertiveness; blue, conceptual; indigo, intuitive; and violet, imaginative. The Hindus believe that if you can open all the chakras simultaneously, the energy centers working in accord with one another, then the spirit is free to leave the body. The individual becomes a being beyond time.

Searching out this phenomenon, I located a book by Raymond Moody entitled *Life After Life*. I felt that this study was completed at a time when it was necessary to help modern man understand his spirituality. Moody interviewed 100 patients who had died and come back to life. While they were dead, they could see themselves lying on the bed. They had gone through a long tunnel or through a cloud, and, in all cases, they had seen a white light or a white figure at the end of the tunnel or cloud. Each was told to return. When they did, their body came back to life.

Modern physics has identified everything in the universe as existing in pairs of opposites. As Capra asserted in *The Tao of Physics*, "Force and matter, particles and waves, motion and rest, existence and non-existence--these are some of the opposite or contradictory concepts which are transcended in modern physics." Fundamental to Jungian psychology is the idea that all pairs are opposites. Dr. Jung said that everything within the psyche is in pairs of opposites. The philosophy that all opposites

40

are polarized--light and dark, contracting and expanding, positive and negative--or are merely different aspects of the same phenomenon, is one of the basic principles of the traditional Oriental perception of the world. Traditional Native American philosophy and thought, too, believes in the duality of everything. Dr. Jung found that the Supreme Being, that which cannot be named, the inconceivable God, is manifest in many forms. These forms appear as pairs of opposites. God is visible and invisible, physical and immaterial, good and bad. He is All in One. He is both. Traditional D/Lakota belief is that Wakan Tanka is one, yet many.

The ancient Christians addressed the feminine element in the divine, thus celebrating God as both male and female. Is this wholistic thought?

In order to maintain wholism, traditional Native American holy people would never say, "I'm a holy man. If you come to me, I'll heal you." It would be the quickest way for them to get themselves out of balance. The usual method used to escape this trap was to have somebody speak on their behalf, another method of staying on the Red Road.

In my lifetime I have witnessed many miracles by Native American holy people, one of which occurred through Frank Fools Crow in 1974. In August of that year, we were having a traditional Lakota fair at Lower Brule, South Dakota, much like the Traditional Sioux Nations Trades Fairs that used to be held every year at the Big Bend on the Missouri River in the mid 1880s, and it was in danger of being closed down because of rainy weather. I remembered reading in D/Lakota history that a long time ago, there were what we call "heyoka," those who had the power to split the clouds and make the storm go around. The traditional Lakota fair was the first effort in many years to renew old ways, old songs, and old dances. All of a sudden, a rainstorm came up and threatened the whole weekend. This is why it was so urgent to ask a heyoka to split the clouds and make the rain go around.

41

I went to a local holy man and asked, "Is there anyone today who still has this power?"

He said, "The medicine people who are heyoka have this power."

I immediately remembered that the evening before at the "wacipi" (Indian dance) a heyoka was dancing. Somebody told me that this heyoka was Frank Fools Crow. I related this information to the local holy man, who told me to get my pipe, load it in a traditional manner, and we would take it to Frank Fools Crow together. This we did.

We offered Frank the pipe in a traditional manner, and then we gave him our request. He told us he could not stop the rain because it was raining for a purpose. "But I could split the clouds," he said, "and I can make the rain go around. So don't worry."

To myself, I puzzled, "How is he going to split these clouds?"

Later, after he had returned the pipe to us, thunder and lightning came around us all that night. But there was no rain! Coincidence or synchronicity?

A story from my Bible training came back to me. Nearly two thousand years ago a holy man lived on the other side of Planet Earth. One day a storm came up and threatened to capsize the boat he was in with his friends. He prayed to God to calm the storm, and it quickly subsided. This is almost identical to what Frank Fools Crow did!

Another miracle I witnessed was on the Hopi reservation in 1967. It took place during the first Hopi ceremony I ever attended. I was taken on top of a mesa at dawn. Everyone had prepared for the ceremony. As I was walking down the narrow streets of the village on top of the mesa, whipper kachinas suddenly came out of the door on the roof of the "kiva." (The kiva is usually built underground in the shape of a cylinder. It is a place for spiritual activities.) They chased and whipped everybody they could catch. The people ran into their homes, closing the doors. Some people ran to their cars, got in and locked the doors. The whipper kachinas whipped the cars, and the people started their vehicles and drove off the mesa.

This was my first time at a ceremony on top of the mesa. I was an Indian, but I felt just like a tourist. I didn't know what was going on. The whipper kachinas started to chase me, trying to whip me. I ran down an alley and around a corner where there was a coal bin with a canvas covering. To escape I jumped into it and covered up with the canvas. I don't know how long I was in hiding. Eventually, it got very quiet. Evidently, the kachinas had gone back into the kiva. I waited a few more minutes, then crawled out of my hiding place.

I came around the corner and looked down toward the other end where I could see the kiva with the ladder sticking out of the door in the center of the roof. I saw Mother Kachina climbing out of the kiva. Coming out, she floated in the air. I knew I was seeing a great miracle. I understood why the whipper kachinas had chased everyone into their homes and off the mesa. At that point I became frightened. I ran to the closest house, flung open the door, and hurried in without even knocking.

Many years later when I was studying the religions of the East, I found a book by Francis Hitching called *The Mysterious World* that told about holy people in India who had the ability to float in the air. That really caused me to think. Hitching also said that the reason Jesus was able to walk on water was that he could levitate, in other words--float. I again remembered my Biblical teachings, in which Jesus said, "Verily, verily, I say unto you, he that believeth on me and the works that I do, shall you do also." Everything that he did, we, too, can do.

Jesus insisted that it was not he who performed the miracles or spoke the teachings, but that God the Father spoke and acted through him. The challenge that Jesus presented to the Pharisees drove the authorities to seek an excuse for his arrest. All they could come up with was that he called himself the son of God.

In my understanding of this concept, it would be much like the Native American holy people of today. They do not say, "I'm a holy man. Come to me, I'll heal you." They would get out of balance. Jesus, likewise, had to speak in such a way that he wouldn't get out of balance. Jesus' means of maintaining balance seems to me to be nearly the same as the Red Road philosophy.

RED ROAD FOR EDUCATIONAL SYNERGY

Synergy is described as combined or cooperative action. Let us apply it to two organs in the body. The two organs referred to in this chapter are the left and right hemispheres of the brain. The Red Road is a wholistic concept; thus the Red Road for educational synergy would be interpreted as a whole-brain approach to education.

The research that has been done on brain hemisphericy states that each side of the brain is dominant in different modes of thought: the left is logical, linear, verbal, abstract, sequential, serial, and masculine thought. The right is instinctive, wholistic, non-verbal, concrete, random, spatial, and feminine thought. Barbara Vitale, in her book *Unicorns are Real: A Right-Brained Approach to Learning*, offers these listings of the brain modes of thought, as well as the skills which follow.

Skills associated with left hemispheric specialization include following directions, reading, writing, detail, reciting, phonetics, and listening. I have been master of ceremonies at many wacipis (pow- wows) throughout the country. I remember one time in Denver, the area where the dancers came in and out of the pow-wow arena was becoming plugged with non-Indians who kept blocking the flow of traffic. As master of ceremonies, I asked them to keep the area clear, but the request went unheard. Realizing that the majority of non Indians are left-brain dominant, I quickly put up a sign that read, "Keep this area clear." As soon as the non-Indians saw the sign, they quickly cleared the area, thus enabling the dancers to go in and out of the arena unhampered.

The right side of the brain also has specialized skills associated with it: creativity, math computation, haptic awareness, music, artistic ability, color sensitivity, visualization.

My research into brain hemisphericy indicated that modern society and our school systems stress the skills and modes of thinking more on the left side of the brain than on the right. Consequently I learned to place emphasis on books and libraries as the sources of all knowledge.

By contrast, in traditional D/Lakota culture, any time a person wanted knowledge or information, he attended a ceremony and requested that information from an iyeska. I learned that in a traditional D/Lakota manner, if one wanted to gain knowledge, he tied an eagle feather onto the spot where the handle and the bowl of the pipe meet. When you use the sacred pipe in a ceremony in this way, you receive knowledge.

In reviewing brain hemisphericy, I concluded that the right hemisphere forms the doorway to the collective unconscious. Any time a person wants information, it's in the collective unconscious portion of the mind.

A hundred years ago D/Lakota people did not have a written language. They did not have books. Any time they wanted knowledge or information, they asked for it ceremonially from the iyeska. Ceremonies were used to find cures for ailments, to interpret dreams, to find things that had been lost, and to look at your past in order to understand your purpose in life as revealed in your vision quest.

Continuing my research, I discovered a book by Thomas Blakeslee entitled *The Right Brain*. He related that there were different right-brain methods of problem solving. One example is thought incubation. He said if you have a thought and the answer doesn't penetrate consciousness, set that thought aside. Don't forget it, just set it aside. Say to yourself, "Later," and it'll come to you. In the traditional D/Lakota way, it is always said, "Think twice before you do something or say something." This statement seems to me to be very similar to Blakeslee's concept of thought incubation.

Another technique for solving problems, Blakeslee remarked, was dream analysis. He asked, "Did you ever go to bed at night with a question on your mind? Then wake with the answer or dream the answer?"

A further example he gave was meditation. One kind is mind-fulness, where you allow any thought to penetrate consciousness, think on it, then let it go. Another thought comes up. You think on it, then let it go. Blakeslee said that creative think tanks around the world use such methods for problem solving.

Fasting to help solve problems was another example put forth by Blakeslee. He stated that Plato, who produced the finest school of philosophy in western civilization, required that his students fast for ten days before they took a test. To me, this is almost the same as traditional D/Lakotas receiving answers while fasting in the vision quest.

Also in the traditional D/Lakota way, you were not allowed to question the elders. You were taught to respect them. The older a person was, the more knowledge he had. You were taught to listen. You were never allowed to ask the question, "Why?" That's the way I grew up. But this traditional concept came into conflict when I went to boarding school. If you didn't raise your hand and ask, "Why?"-- questioning everything--you usually ended up with a "D" or an "F."

About ten years ago I attended a workshop in Denver called "Balancing the Brain." The presentor, Dr. William Boast, told the participants at the beginning of his workshop, "I'm not going to allow you to ask any questions in this workshop. I'm also going to frown upon anybody who takes notes at any great length." He continued, "For every question you have, the answer is right here." And he pointed to his head. He said that man has to begin reorganizing his thinking, "And you might as well start now while you're in this workshop!" He added, "Don't worry if you have questions. The answers will come to you in their own time." I found these ideas reinforcing to the traditional D/Lakota way, making me feel good about the workshop.

In reading a book on Indian education, *Speaking of Indians* by Ella Deloria, I discovered that a traditional D/Lakota mode of edu cating was through example. Children learned by someone set-

47

ting an example for them. For instance, when a young boy came of age, his uncle or grandfather usually took him along on the hunt. The boy followed along and just watched. Maybe a whole year went by. He was taken along on many different activities, and only later allowed to attempt the task at hand.

Blakeslee commented that a delivery method allowing the right side of the brain to function as a doorway to the collective unconscious is that of learning through discovery. By permitting the child to discover his own answer, his understanding and retention of that experience are much greater. Once again, I was thrilled by this explanation; it was exactly the same as the traditional D/Lakota way of learning through precept and example.

Other examples of right-brain activities offered by Blakeslee were visual aids, diagrams, charts, key words, and phrases. When I came across the word phrases, I remembered in *A Story of Jesus, Based on the Edgar Cayce Readings* compiled by Clifford P. Owens that the only time the Master wrote, he used a phrase to teach the people. Was Jesus a right-hemispheric dominant person? He wrote no term papers or theses. As a matter of fact, his occupation was that of a carpenter, one which largely utilizes right-brain functions.

Respect for each individual is a traditional D/Lakota value. In the old way when a woman married a man, she did not take his name but kept her own name. If they had four children, the children did not take the man's name either. They each received their own names. The common name was the "tiospaye" or clan name. But then somebody came across the ocean and said, "Don't believe that, you Indian women. When you get married, you gotta take the man's name. Now you're Mrs. Chuck Ross, and you'd better obey!" Once again, I could see how these two examples are related to brain hemisphericy, the left side being masculine in its expression and the right side being feminine in its expression.

About twenty years ago a renaissance started in Native American philosophy and thought. More and more people recognize and respect people's individuality. There is a movement toward a more wholistic, balanced society. This respect for individuals in traditional D/Lakota society carried over into their education. In the old days, we didn't have separate classes for slow learners. If a person was slow, we just worked with him or her a little bit more.

A current educational concept which incorporates this respect for the individual is called individualized instruction. The student is graded on personal achievements with the idea that each child has his or her own learning rate. This method is not very popular in educational circles because it requires work for the teachers. They have to develop pre- and post-tests for each course and for each student. Most teachers, therefore, usually grade students in a group. They call it grading on the curve. To me, grading on the curve only indicates a student's place in comparison with others, rather than a place with one's own achievements. Individualized or small-group instruction is more beneficial for the student but seems to be unpopular for institutions because of the extra effort teachers need to put forth.

Thomas Blakeslee also expounded on test development. He stressed that tests don't always have to be written. They can be individualized and can come in various forms: as a product, a demonstration, an illustration, or even an oral presentation. Such testing alternatives are excellent for allowing a more whole-brain approach to education.

Storytelling was used in traditional D/Lakota education. The "teacher" would tell a story with a strong moral value. (Dr. Boast had said, in his workshop, that all learning occurs when one is in brain-wave pattern alpha and that the best way to get a child into the alpha brain-wave pattern was to tell him a story.)

In completing more research on this topic, I found that meditation was a method for solving problems. In the East, the Buddhists teach by using koans, which are riddles meant to help the student realize the limitations of logic and reasoning. The irrational wording and paradoxical content of these riddles makes it impossible to solve them by thinking. The student has to meditate on the riddles and allow the answer to come up from the collective unconscious. One of the most famous koans used by the Zen masters in teaching is, "What is the sound of one hand clapping?" It doesn't make any sense to me, but I imagine a person would have to meditate on the question in order to find his own answer.

After studying the koan system of teaching, I recalled my Biblical teachings where it was said about Jesus, "He called them unto him and he said unto them a parable, 'How can Satan cast out Satan?'" That sounded like a koan to me. I wondered how you solved these parables, these riddles. Does one have to meditate on them, like the Buddhists, in order to solve them?

Dr. Jung declared that when you are born, all that exists at that moment is the collective unconscious. From that time forward, your consciousness starts to develop. Therefore, I considered, children in early childhood must be whole-brain learners. They would be more in balance and, consequently, be in contact with the collective unconscious. In the past twenty years of my involvement in Indian education, I have noticed that Indian children in the younger grades do well; they're on a par with the rest of the nation's students. When they reach sixth or seventh grade, however, there's a sudden tapering off or a drop in their learning and test scores. I thought about this and asked the question, "Is it because our children are right-brain learners and the instruction is geared mainly to the left- brain learner?" As mentioned previously, Dr. Jung stated that a person's consciousness starts developing at birth; the conscious breaks away from the unconscious at puberty. I understand this to mean that younger children are whole-brain learners, while after puberty they become dominant in one hemisphere or the other as dictated by their culture. In the case of American Indians, a majority would be right-brain dominant.

Continuing this line of thought, I remember that Jesus said, "Suffer the little children to come unto me and forbid them not. For of such is the kingdom of God." I take the meaning of this to be that young children are still in contact with the kingdom of God. D/Lakota people say that newborns are still at their spirit level. Dr. Jung said that these young ones are still in contact with the collective unconscious. I thus question, "Is the kingdom of God the same as the collective unconscious?"

In *Supersensonics: The Science of Radiational Paraphysics* by Dr. Christopher Hills, he declared that the kingdom of God is, indeed, the collective unconscious, and Thomas Blakeslee said that the doorway to the collective unconscious is the right hemisphere of the brain. Blakeslee also remarked that the brain is like a computer. It stores everything it sees and hears. The trick is how to recall the information. If you want to bring it up with a computer, you just hit "menu." The human brain, according to Blakeslee, brings up information through pictures, symbols, key words, and diagrams. These are recall methods for information that is stored within the brain.

Once a woman came up to me and said, "How in the world did you memorize the ten lectures in your series? You must have a remarkable memory!" I told her I don't memorize anything, that I use pictures, slides, and diagrams. The moment an image comes on the screen, instant recall of the story is connected to that picture.

The traditional D/Lakota way of record-keeping was through pictures. The people kept a winter count, on which they drew one picture per year. The most important event of the year was drawn in the picture. The person seeing that picture for a certain year was immediately able to recall information about that whole year. These pictures on the winter count were painted in a spiral form, starting in the center and coming out clockwise--one symbol per year.

I would like to demonstrate a little exercise I learned in a Pacific Institute workshop on how the brain functions with the use of symbols. Read the sentence below and count the number of "f's." Give yourself 20 seconds.

FINISHED FILES ARE THE RE-
SULT OF YEARS OF SCIENTIF-
IC STUDY COMBINED WITH THE
EXPERIENCE OF MANY YEARS.

Normally, when someone finishes reading this sentence, they have counted three "f's." A few individuals can see four, five, or even six "f's." There are six "f's" in this sentence. They are located in "finished," "files," and "scientific," and the three "of's." Now go back and read through the sentence again to see if you can find the six "f's."

To explain what might be going on in this scenario: when I said to look for the symbol "f," right away in our minds we thought of the sound of "f" as in "finished," "files, "scientific." But in "of," the sound is not an "f;" it is a "v" sound. You look right at it and still can't see it because you're looking for the sound of "f." The first time I did this exercise, I could see only three "f's." When the instructor in one of my classes told us there were six "f's," I got angry with him, thinking he was playing a trick on us.

Later, when I was studying Jungian psychology, I found that when a person can admit his weakness, no matter what it is, that process is called individuation. If a person can admit they're a left-brain thinker and out of balance, that is known as the process of individuation. Jung said that the conscious coming to terms with the inner self generally starts with the ego being wounded and with the suffering that goes along with that pain.

Another example of individuation is when I had to come to terms with myself about being an alcoholic. I could not admit it for years, but once I conceded that I was an alcoholic, that was a wounding of my ego and I had to suffer the consequences. Individuation is the first step to transcendent function. Dr. Jung said that transcendent function is being whole or being in balance. If we can admit that the English language is a left-brain language and is out of balance, that's the process of individuation. There's nothing wrong with that.

Dr. William Boast stated that a more balanced approach to teaching reading was through the use of MGuffey's readers because the emphasis was on teaching sounds to groups of letters rather than to individual letters. As an example, the word "reader" is divided into two parts by McGuffey--as "read-er." The McGuffey's readers divided the word "eclectic" into three parts-- "ec-lec-tic."

The Chinese language has an ideogramic structure. That means they use a symbol for a word or a whole thought. In a diagram taken from *Tao: The Watercourse Way* by Alan W. Watts and Chung Liang-Huang, the symbols on one side of the page are original symbols in Chinese; those on the other side are the English equivalents; the symbols in the middle of the page show the evolutionary development of the Chinese symbols. There is a symbol for "sheep" in the left-hand column. When you see this symbol, the first thing that comes to mind is "sheep," the animal. In the same column is the symbol "mountain." Immediately, a physical mountain comes to mind.

The English equivalents in the right-hand column look quite different. For example, the word "mountain" has eight symbols. The way the word is being taught is that each symbol has its own sound. When the child looks at the word, he sounds it out: M O - "mow," U N - "mow-un," T A - "mow-un-ta," I N - "mow-un-ta-in,"--"mountain." By the time you figure out how to say the word mountain, you forgot what a mountain was! In an ideogramic language, when you see the symbol for mountain, you instantly know it's a mountain.

Today as I drive down the highway and look around, I notice all types of ideogramic symbols in our modern culture. When you see the symbol "Taco Bell," you know right away it's a place to eat Mexican food. The McDonald's arches let you know it's a place where you get the Big Mac. Sales people have been using ideogramic symbols to help sell their products for years and years. The media--TV, computers, videos--also use symbols to get their message across.

One of the most common ideogramic symbols is road signs. The symbol for stop, the red hexagon, is almost universal. When you see the symbol, you know it means to stop, whether you can read the words or not.

Author Alan Watts advocated the teaching of Chinese in secondary schools, not only because we must learn how to communicate with the Chinese, but also because of all high cultures in the world, theirs is most different from ours (American) in its ways of thinking. He stated that every culture is based on assumptions so taken for granted that they are barely conscious. It is only when we study these highly different cultures and languages that we become fully aware of them. I pondered what he was trying to say and wondered if his message was, "Do we need to take a look at other people in their culture and develop respect for them?"

Once again, I'd like to share a personal example in this area. My first marriage was to a Hopi woman. I didn't really think about it, but I assumed that Indians are Indians and that we ought to be able to get along. Yet Pat and I ended up fighting like cats and dogs. I remember my confusion at what was happening to me in not being able to put a finger on what I should do in these difficult situations. I decided to study the Hopis to get a better idea of how they thought. What I learned first was that the Hopis are matriarchal. The woman is the head of the clan. She owns the home, she owns the fields, and she owns the sheep.

I grew up with the Oglalas, who were patriarchs. A hunting culture, the man was the head of the societies. The more I studied

54

my former wife's culture and her people, the more I learned about myself. I believe this is what Alan Watts was trying to say when he advocated learning Chinese. In the process of learning another culture, you learn just as much about yourself and how you are a part of your culture. I recognized this as another way of working with the process of individuation and as a step toward transcendent function.

Watts went on to say that standard European languages like English and French have sentences structured so that the verb must be set in motion by the noun, thereby presenting metaphysical problems as meaningless. He said that you cannot solve metaphysical problems by using standard European languages. In order to solve a metaphysical problem, one needs to meditate on that problem and allow the symbols of the unconscious to penetrate consciousness. Dr. Jung said that modern man needs to learn the language of the unconscious.

Japanese prepositional phrases are the opposite of English phrases. The sentence, "The book on the desk" becomes "desk upon book" in saying it the way a Japanese person would. In Japanese sentence structure, verbs come at the ends of sentences. Thinking about this, I recognized a similarity between the structures of Japanese and the Dakota/Lakota languages. A simple Lakota sentence is, "Tatanka wahanpi kagayo." Translated into English, it says, "Buffalo stew make." The verb comes last, at the end of the sentence. Verbs in the Dakota/Lakota language structures come at the end of the sentence. In the structure of English, the sentence would read, "Make the buffalo stew." English is backwards!

Many linguistics scholars have been impressed with the dominance of the verb in American Indian sentences and by the fact that the verb is more oriented to the object than to the subject. This leads one to assume that the American Indian is more interested in the result than in the cause. It appears that people who are oriented toward the cause of an event would be more left-brain-dominant, and those interested in results would have more of a right-brain-dominance.

Was Leonardo da Vinci right-brain dominant? He was five hundred years ahead of his time in his accomplishments and inventions. He was a painter, a sculptor, a mathematician, and an astronomer. He designed aircraft, parachutes, and self-propelled wheeled vehicles. In reviewing a page from his notebook, I discovered that he wrote his sentences from right to left--backwards in mirror writing. In order to read his notebook, the average person had to hold it up to a mirror.

I wanted to experiment with da Vinci's writing habits. I wrote the simple sentence, "Make the buffalo stew." backwards in mirror writing. When I held it up to a mirror, I discovered it said, "Stew buffalo the make." That's exactly how the D/Lakota language is structured: starting with the subject, adding the descriptive word, and placing the verb last. Earlier I pointed out that American Indian language structure allowed the right side of the brain to function. My questions then became, "Did Leonardo da Vinci's mind function in such a way? Did he utilize this doorway to the collective unconscious? Is this the reason he was five hundred years ahead of his time?" I feel the majority of people are "book" people. I'm a book person. All I know is what I read in the library. But it appears that Leonardo da Vinci's creativity came to him from the collective unconscious.

Further research into the Dakota/Lakota language structures, in *Oglala Religion* by William K. Powers, identified that separate lexical categories are not employed to differentiate between time and space. Time and space are inseparable. All temporal statements in the Dakota/Lakota languages are simultaneously spatial. Example: A simple sentence in Lakota is, "Letan Pine Ridge towhan hwo." The literal English interpretation is, "When is Pine Ridge from here?" But in the English language, the same sentence is usually stated, "How far is it to Pine Ridge?", indicating

56

left-brain dominance. Thus, in the Lakota language, the spatial or right-brain orientation is dominant.

Marilyn Ferguson said in *The Aquarian Conspiracy* that European languages trap us in a model of understanding that is piecemeal. They pay no attention to relationships by their subject/predicate structure, thus molding our thought patterns by making us think in terms of simple cause and effect. She further stated that, "...for this reason it is hard for us to talk about or even think about quantum physics, the fourth dimension, or any other notion without clear-cut beginning and ending, up and down, then and now."

Modern science has discovered that there is something in the cosmos that is not in accord with the concepts that modern man has formed. Charlton Laird's book *Language in America* recorded that linguist Benjamin Whorf suggested that the Hopi language, if it will not help scientists find a new language they need, may at least help them see what is wrong with the old one. My interpretation of this is that Native American languages allow more right-brain expression, whereas European languages encourage almost solely left-brain expression.

A Hopi prophecy told about two brothers--a white one and a red one. The white brother went to the other side of the planet and will return one day. When he comes back, the two brothers will sit down together and learn each other's language. After that, their two lifeways will entwine and become one.

When I heard this prophecy, what first occurred to me was the information about the left and right hemispheres of the brain. To me, the white brother would be left-brain dominant, and the red brother would be right-brain dominant because of their differing language structures. After we learn each other's ways, we will become whole-brain thinkers. Marilyn Ferguson commented that the joining of the two hemispheres creates something new. Whole-brain knowing is more than the sum of its parts and different from either, she said.

Balance, or the Red Road philosophy, is a key to whole-brain knowing. Blakeslee felt that in using the functions of the right side of the brain, one would be able to make contact with the collective unconscious. Carl Jung believed that any time knowledge or informa tion was wanted, it was contained within the collective unconscious portion of the mind.

A man who had a natural ability to make contact with the collective unconscious was Edgar Cayce. He was a spiritual healer. People who had incurable diseases went to him for help. He would enter into a self-meditative state, making contact with the collective unconscious. Then he would "iyeska" the information from that part of the mind, offering diagnoses and natural remedies for the healing of the sick person. Under normal conditions, Cayce had no knowledge of medicinal cures.

I was astounded that the method Edgar Cayce used to receive information was almost identical to those used by traditional D/Lakotas and other Native American holy people.

Additional similarities, besides those dealing with healing techniques, exist. For instance, both the information from the collective unconscious of Edgar Cayce and that from the myths of Native Americans declare that Native Americans have always been in North America. In researching Native American origin stories, I did not find one story stating that American Indians came across the Bering Straits.

Carl Jung remarked that myths from all cultures contain substance and that they originate in the collective unconscious. One of the Native American oral histories states that the people originated in North America. The information coming from the collective unconscious of Edgar Cayce said that the red man appeared in North America ten million years ago.

Recently, a skull was found off the coastal cliffs of San Diego. The scientists called this skull Del Mar Man. When a carbon-14 dating test was done, the skull could not be dated because it was too old. Now there is a new way of measuring the age of bones,

58

called acid racemization. The age is determined by measuring the age of the amino acids in the bone. This method was used on the skull of Del Mar Man. The results showed that that skull was almost 50,000 years old! When I read this, I questioned, "How in the world did he get over here? That's 20,000 years before the Bering Straits even opened up." Maybe the origin myths of the Native Americans are true after all!

Sitting Bull, who tried to get the non-Indians to accept his culture, stated shortly before his death that if a man loses something and goes back to look carefully for it, he will find it. This is what I feel the American Indians are doing today in reclaiming the validity of their own culture. It's all a part of the renaissance in American Indian philosophy and thought.

ORIGINS OF THE RED MAN PART I: ATLANTIS

Twenty-five years ago I started on a search for my roots, a search for the origins of my tribe. Looking for the origins of my own tribe, I synchronistically discovered five origin legends: the legend that Native Americans originated in North America; the legend that they emerged from the underground; the legend that they came from an island in the east; the legend that they came from the stars; and the legend that they came from an island in the west. Many tribes claim one or more of these legends. The tribes of the Dakota Nation have the first four among their historical stories. I would like to share this search for my roots.

My grandmother used to tell us that the Mdewakantonwan was the mother tribe and that we were the first people on earth. I discovered later that many other tribes have a very similar story. I patronized a local pub called the Viking Bar when I attended the University of Minnesota. One day I met a couple of boys from the Winnebago tribe there. We sat down together and began to swap stories about our history and culture. Very proudly, I declared to them, "My grandma told me we were the first tribe on earth." One of them said, "Hey, wait a minute. My grandma told me that *we* were the first." Soon we were standing and hollering at each other about who was the first tribe on earth!

Continuing my investigation of the origin stories of the Mdewakantonwan, I learned that the Mdewakantonwan came from an island in the east. In trying to pinpoint where this island was, my reaction was that we must have come from an island in the Great Lakes, since my grandmother told me that as a young child, she had lived in Minnesota.

Reading more, I learned that the language of the Dakota people came from a larger group called the Siouan linguistic stock. I discovered that there are 36 different tribes which are part of this same linguistic stock.

I compared origin stories with many of these tribes, and became aware that they were similar. The stories indicated that they came from the east, from under the water in the east, or from an island in the east. The anthropology of the Dakota people determined that they were located in North Carolina about 1400 A.D. This made my thoughts on the origins shift from the Great Lakes to the area east of the East Coast. I also found that other tribes, besides those from the Siouan linguistic stock, had origin stories about coming from an island in the east. The Mayans have an origin story that says they came from an island in the east which sank into the ocean. Before it sank, many of the people came to the Americas. Is this sunken island perhaps a reference to the Dakota origin story of coming from under the water in the east?

One day as I was browsing through a bookstore, a particular book seemed to be illuminated in a flash of light, standing out from all the rest. I reached for it, pulled it out, and saw that it was entitled *Edgar Cayce on Atlantis* by Edgar Evans Cayce. Cayce did an incredible amount of research presenting evidence to support the theory of Atlantis.

After reading this book, I got more interested in the possibilities of an Atlantis. I found out, through further study, about a professor who used to teach ancient literature at the Air Force Academy. He became acquainted with Plato's writings about an island called Atlantis. He grew so intrigued with the idea of a sunken continent that he quit his job at the Air Force Academy and went on an expedition looking for indications of the existence of this continent. He found evidence of a sunken city off the shores of the Bimini Islands, which he describes in his book *Stones of Atlantis*. This man's name is Dr. David Zink.

Researching Atlantis more fully, I uncovered information about a petroglyph which was thought to be 50,000 years old. It was found in Ica, Peru and displayed a map which identified North America, South America, and a very large island in the Atlantic

Ocean. Is this evidence of an island that used to exist in the Atlantic which might have sunk?

Another study presented in Zink's book was by a Frenchman named Dr. Piggott who took core drillings of the soil on the ocean floor. These drillings were done in a line from New York to England. In the middle of the Atlantic he found volcanic ash in the core. The ash, he determined, could not have been formed underwater. It had to have been formed in open air! His theory was that at one time this part of the ocean floor was above the water.

Poring over the books on Atlantis, I could see that many of the writers felt the people of Atlantis had migrated east and west from Atlantis to civilize the world. Some went to Europe, others to America. They came out from Atlantis in two directions. In my way of thinking, if this was true, there should be similarities on both sides of the Atlantic that would corroborate this migration pattern.

I perused *America B.C.* by Barry Fell, a linguistics specialist. He learned that the Micmac Indians of Canada are related linguistically to the Egyptians. The Algonquin-speaking peoples are related to the Celts and Basques. The Zunis have a linguistic relationship to the Libyans, and the Pimas to the Iberic-speaking peoples. Fell's hypothesis is that ancient people sailed across the Atlantic to America in pre-Columbus times. My thought, however, was, "Maybe the connections for these linguistic similarities came from Atlantis."

Charles Berlitz, who speaks 33 different languages and is the grandson of the Berlitz who started the Berlitz School of Languages, stated in *The Mystery of Atlantis* that people of the Siouan linguistic stock were related linguistically to the Rumanian and Turkish-speaking people. The strongest evidence for the existence of an Atlantis was the linguistic studies reported in his book.

In *America B.C.*, Barry Fell wrote of the discovery of ancient hieroglyphics of the Micmac Indians in Canada which, when compared with Egyptian hieroglyphics, were very similar and in some cases identical. Dr. Fell indicated this to be evidence that ancient Egyptians traveled to Canada, but the people who believe in Atlantis feel it to be evidence that the ideas came from the island and went in two different directions.

I decided to see if there were other cross-Atlantic similarities besides linguistic ones. Among the D/Lakota people, a traditional headpiece which the dancers wore is called a roach. This headpiece was received when a young man was initiated into a society. I checked with other tribes that were part of the Siouan linguistic stock and found that they, too, had a similar headpiece. I realized, also, that they, like the D/Lakota, received this roach when they were initiated into their traditional societies.

Then I reviewed the ancient cultures of Europe and discovered that the Greeks of antiquity received a very similar headpiece when they were initiated into their societies. In Rome the ancient Etruscans received a like headpiece when they were initiated into their societies. Where did this idea come from?

Additional cultural evidence for the existence of Atlantis was found in pottery designs. Dr. Fell uncovered such designs that he believed had a common influence from both the Celtic civilization and from Panama. There are also commonalities between pottery from the ancient Minoan civilization and that of Acoma Pueblo in New Mexico. Why are they so much the same? Coincidence? Or synchronicity?

I discovered, in comparing additional cultural items, that the basket design of the Pima Indians of Arizona can be found among the Hopi. The Hopi call the symbol in the design the emergence symbol. On the other side of the Atlantic, the same symbol was found on the ancient island of Crete, stamped on a coin. It was also found on Persian designs of old. How did it get there? Why is it the same as ours?

Stonehenge is in England. It wasn't until recently that scientists realized this site was a giant astronomical calendar. The ancients used it to tell the longest day, the shortest day, and when day and night are equal. There is some speculation by scientists that this site was also used as a star calendar.

I learned there is also a Stonehenge in America, located at Mystery Hill, New Hampshire. The stones at this site are also aligned to tell the longest day, the shortest day, the fall and spring equi noxes. Where did these ideas come from? Maybe ancient Indians went to England to build Stonehenge and then returned. I don't know. The Atlantean theorists feel that these ideas came from Atlantis.

In 1975 an artist, Anna Sofaer, "accidentally" discovered an astronomical calendar in Chaco Canyon, New Mexico. On the Summer Solstice (the longest day of the year), she had been sitting on the rim overlooking the canyon. She noticed a giant spiral etched into the rock below her in the shadows of a crevice. The sunlight came through the crevice at an angle, producing a sliver of light which she called the Sun Dagger. It then moved to the center of the spiral and stopped. Was the discovery of this sun dagger coincidence or was it a synchronistic event? Anthropologists are now re-evaluating the knowledge of the primitive Indians and are speculating that the ancient Americans were more sophisticated than once thought.

The Hopi Indians today still use the longest day, the shortest day and the two equinoxes to mark the time of their ceremonies through the use of natural landmarks. For instance, looking westward from Second Mesa, Arizona on the shortest day of the year, one notices the sun setting on the slope of one of the lower peaks of the San Francisco Mountains near Flagstaff. The Winter Solstice is the starting point for the Hopi ceremonial year. The kachinas return at that time.

For the D/Lakota people the Summer Solstice has had religious significance. Traditionally, on the first full moon after the longest day, the Sun Dance was held.

I found that the Inca Indians of Peru also acknowledged the sun on the longest day. The old Celtic civilization, as well, acknowledged the sun in a sacred manner. They had a sun god they called Baal. And the ancient Egyptians acknowledged the sun in a sacred way. Their sun god was called Aton. The Germanic-speaking peoples in Europe of olden times honored the sun in a sacred manner. Anthropologists have discovered that these people carried, in a sun wagon, a gold disk representing the sun. How did so many cultures get the same idea? Where did it come from?

In old France a sun altar with a sun sign on it was found. The estimated age is thought to be approximately 7,000 years old. When I saw a photograph of this sun sign, it looked exactly like a D/Lakota medicine wheel. We still use the medicine wheel in a sacred manner in our ceremonies today.

The ancient Etruscans of Italy had an identical design to the medicine wheel. It was used in their philosophy that there is no such thing as pure chance or coincidence. They believed that everything was a result of supernatural law. Traditional D/Lakota philosophy and thought has the same belief.

The Hopis, when they have their sacred Snake Dance, use the medicine wheel symbol painted on the ground. Snakes, messengers for the prayers of the people, are released after the prayers are delivered. The snakes carry the prayers back into Mother Earth. Modern man doesn't understand the Hopi Snake Dance; many think the people worship snakes. But that is not the case. The snake is simply the messenger to carry the prayers into the heart of Mother Earth.

The medicine wheel symbol can be found on tombstones in Basque cemeteries located in the Pyrenees Mountains of Spain. The same symbol can be found in the ancient Celtic civilization. It is known as the Celtic cross. Identical symbols on both sides of the Atlantic Ocean! Did these ideas originate in Atlantis?

During my school days, I was taught about giant pyramids located in Egypt. It wasn't until later on in life that I discovered there are pyramids in the Americas too--in Guatemala, Honduras, and

Mexico. They were part of the ancient Mayan civilization. There's a pyramid a few miles from Mexico City called the Pyramid of the Sun, the land base of which is bigger than the largest pyramid in Egypt.

The largest man-made structure in the history of the world, though, is situated a few miles east of St. Louis, Missouri. Originally, it was thought to have been built in the shape of a pyramid but over the years, various weather conditions and erosion have caused it to look like a giant hill. This site is known as Kahokia. An ancient astronomical calendar marking the longest day, the shortest day, and when day and night are equal was found there. Anthropologists have determined that the natives used this kind of instrument to tell them when to plant and harvest their crops. They felt the calendar was entirely agriculturally-related. I feel, however, that it was spiritually-related because personal experience has shown me that the astronomical calendars were used to tell the people when the cosmic energy was just right for them to initiate their prayers.

A tremendous number of mounds have been discovered in the eastern part of the United States. Some of them apparently originally had a pyramid shape, but the vast majority were cone-shaped. What first entered my mind when I thought of the cone shape was that many of the original homes of Native Americans were built in this shape. I had seen drawings of early woodland Indians who had cone-shaped homes made of birch bark. Plains Indians used cone-shaped homes made from animal skins. Even the original Navajo hogans were cone-shaped.

The tipi, the cone-shaped home of the Plains Indians, was considered a church as well as a home. The altar was originally placed in the center of the floor right below the apex of the tipi poles. Hollywood built a fireplace there, and the tradition has continued, the altar having disappeared from the center of the tipi.

In *Pyramid Power*, Max Toth and Greg Nielsen stated that an invisible power exists at a certain level within the pyramid which enhances longevity and creates a continuum of energy. They also said that this same power exists within the cone. I thought, "Is this the reason the ancients had their altar in the center of the tipi? Is this the reason that originally their home was also their church?" Many artifacts were discovered when the mounds in the eastern part of the United States were excavated. In the Spiral Mound of Oklahoma, anthropologists found a deer mask with horns. A mask almost exactly like it was also discovered in ancient France. Otto Muck, author of *Secrets of Atlantis*, compared these two deer masks and observed that they were almost identical. His hypothesis was that the idea for these masks must have originated in Atlantis. He also compared bronze spearheads found in Massachusetts and in Spain. Likewise, he hypothesized that the idea for these identical spearheads originated in Atlantis. When I was going to school, I was taught that the ancient Indians were of the Stone Age and did not have metal. Now there is evidence that supports the idea that the ancient Indians did, indeed, have metal.

In Etowah Mound, Georgia, several statues were found that were colored red, white, and black. Plato, in his writings on Atlantis, said that the basic colors on Atlantis were red, white, and black. In fact, he commented, these were the colors the people of Atlantis painted their homes. Coincidence? Or synchronicity?

Further research on evidence for the existence of Atlantis turned up a picture of a mummy casket of a pharaoh from ancient Egypt. Examining the photo, I noticed that the pharaoh's hair was tied in a knot in the back. I recognized this arrangement to be like a statue found in a mound located in Kentucky. Comparing these hairstyles, I also noted that the Navajo Indians today still wear their hair tied in a knot in the back when they are in their spiritual training. The Hopi traditional kiva leaders, too, wear their hair knotted in the back to this day.

My search returned to Europe as I continued to look for similar hairstyles. In a book on ancient Mesopotamia, I found evidence of people who used to tie their hair in a knot in the back--4000 years ago.

Charles Berlitz told in his book on Atlantis of the discovery of a statue from pre-Hispanic Spain which he felt was sculpted by a man who had been to Atlantis or had talked to someone from Atlantis. The statue is of a woman who has her hair formed into a wheel on each side of the head. Berlitz called this statue the Priestess of Atlantis. In seeing a picture of this statue, I immediately recognized the hairstyle as a traditional ceremonial hairstyle for Hopi maidens. Where did this idea originate? In Atlantis? Why are these two hair styles from such different parts of the world the same? Coincidental? Or synchronistic?

Dr. Otto Muck said that Atlantis was the center of the world. He further stated that the red-skinned man inhabited Atlantis and that it was the red-skinned man who came out from Atlantis to settle the world.

The comparison among artifacts that may have originated in Atlantis continues. The D/Lakota people used a method to record their history by painting one symbol per year on a buffalo hide. This was called a winter count. The painting started with a symbol in the center of the hide, and each additional symbol then expanded in a counter-clockwise circle. This same idea was used by only one other tribe, the Kiowa.

Yet on the other side of the Atlantic on the Mediterranean island of Crete, an ancient stone calendar was found that has symbols expanding from the center in a counter-clockwise circle--identical in style to the D/Lakota winter count. In ancient Italy as well, a stone calendar of the Etruscans was discovered with the same method of recording the information.

In another example, when I was living in the Hopi Pueblo and studying their ancient culture, I found that they never plowed the ground to plant their crops. They used a stick. They just poked a hole in the ground and put the seed in the hole. Looking into this idea further, I discovered that it was also used by the ancient

HOPI　　　　　　**NAVAJO**　　　　　　**SUMERIAN**

Is it coincidence? or synchronistic? that an overwhelming amount of similarities lead to Atlantis as an origin location.

Left   Right

Priestess of Atlantis   Hopi maiden in ceremonial head dress

Did the culture of the Hopi influence the Atlanteans?

Inca Indians of South America. Additionally, the book *Secrets of Atlantis* referred to this method of planting by using a stick to loosen the soil. It is still used by the Basques of Spain today. Where did they get this idea? Why is it the same as ours?

Dr. Louis Spence, in Berlitz' book *The Mystery of Atlantis*, hypothesized that the people of Atlantis came out in different migratory periods. He stated that the first people to migrate from Atlantis to Europe and America were those of Cro-Magnon Man. This migration was about 25,000 B.C. The next migration from Atlantis to Europe and America was the Magdalena Man, about 14,000 B.C. In the final migration from Atlantis to Europe and America was Azilian Man, about 10,000 B.C.

Upon reading this, my mind flashed back to Otto Muck's book on Atlantis in which he said that Neanderthal Man of Europe was conquered by Cro-Magnon Man, and that Cro-Magnon Man had come from the west. Dr. Muck remarked that Cro-Magnon Man was a red-skinned person. He verified this statement by doing a study of skeletal structures of Cro-Magnon Man and ancient Lakota people.

Once when I was giving a lecture to a group of Lakota high school students and pointed out this comparison to them, their reaction was, "What are you trying to tell us, that we're cave men?"

I said, "No. In fact, research on Cro-Magnon Man by Robert Stacy Judd indicated that Cro-Magnon Man was the most intelligent of all ancient men and was the largest in physical stature." I told the group that this puts a different light on the ancient Lakota Indians. If we are, indeed, related to Cro-Magnon Man, then we come from a highly intelligent human specimen.

Comparing different language groups in North America, I discovered that there are basically four linguistic groups which contain over 2000 different languages. Additional research indicated that there are another 2000 languages located in South America. Morris Swedish, a linguistics specialist, declared that it would take at least 3500 years for one language to separate into two distinct

71

languages. My mind began working on the problem of how long it would take for 4000 languages to come into existence at this rate. I concluded that it would have taken over 50,000 years. That's 30,000 years before the Bering Straits ever opened up!

If American Indians came across the Bering Straits, then it seems to me that, based on Swedish's findings, many different tribes all had to cross the Straits at the same time. Or the Bering Straits theory is not a viable one for the origins of the red man in the Americas. Currently a polarization exists among anthropologists on the Bering Straits theory. More and more are finding new evidence which supports the theory that man originated in the Americas. On the other hand, more and more anthropologists are running to the Bering Straits searching for further evidence to keep their theory alive! Meanwhile, Native Americans are watching this clash over the Bering Straits theory when we know, from our oral histories, that we were always in North America.

Earlier, I mentioned that Edgar Cayce had the natural ability to make contact with his collective unconscious. He achieved this by going into a self-meditative state. While he was in this altered state of consciousness, the collective unconscious would speak through him. On several occasions, the voice of Cayce's collective unconscious stated that the red man had appeared in two places on this planet, North America and Atlantis. When I read this, I said to myself, "That's identical to Dakota oral history."

The tribe I am a member of, the Mdewakantowan, has an oral history that says we came from an island in the east. My wife, who is a member of the Oglala tribe, also talks about an oral history which says they originated in the Black Hills. We have stories that are identical to those coming from the collective unconscious of Cayce. Is it coincidence or synchronicity that these stories are identical?

The literature about Atlantis estimated that the island sank about 10,000 years ago. Before it sank, however, people on the island were warned. Those who heeded the warning left and came to North America to join their red brothers. Information from Cayce's altered state reported that one of the migrations from Atlantis to North America was approximately 15,000 B.C. Reading this, I recalled a book entitled *The Sioux Trail* by John Upton Terrell, who had traced the roots of the Siouan linguistic speaking peoples. In his book, he presented evidence of those peoples originating in North Carolina approximately 15,000 B.C. They slowly migrated northwestward until eventually they reached the Dakotas. Is it really a coincidence that the appearance of the Siouan people in North Carolina is the same date that Cayce said they left Atlantis?

Such information is contrary to many modern beliefs that all American Indians came through the Bering Straits. I do not doubt that some people may have migrated across the Bering Straits; when you look at the top of the world, the Eskimos appear on both sides of the Bering Straits. They may be the ones who used the Bering Straits, and they still live there today.

Charles Berlitz stated, in *The Mystery of Atlantis* that between the Azores (a group of Portuguese islands) and West Africa, another group of islands, the Canary Islands, exists. He said that when the Portuguese first arrived on these islands, they found people there. The Portuguese wondered how these people had gotten to the islands because they had no boats. In questioning the natives, the Portuguese discovered that the inhabitants used a system of government which had ten kings.

When I heard this, I was reminded of the story by Plato who said that the first man on Atlantis was Poseidon. His wife's name was Cleito. Together, they had five sets of male twins who became the ruling kings of Atlantis. This is nearly the same as the story that the Portuguese found among the native people on the Canary Islands. Did those people originate in the Canary Islands? Is that why they didn't have boats?

Evidence from the collective unconscious places Atlantis at this location

Poseidon's symbol was the trident, pictured as a fork with three tines on it. That symbol can be found on traditional D/Lakota pipe bags, and it represents purity. It can be found on traditional D/Lakota cradle boards, again representing purity. When a new-born comes into the world, he is pure. Thus, the trident design would be beaded onto the cradle board. Did elements of the D/Lakota people originate in Atlantis? Is this why the D/Lakota people used this trident symbol?

In researching certain symbology of other tribes, I found that the trident symbol is found on the headpiece of the Apache crown dancers. Actually, the Apaches say that the original name for the crown dancers was the spirit mountain dancers. Their oral history of the spirit mountain dancers was that they came from mountains in the east.

As I continued my investigations, I found information showing a giant trident symbol etched into the side of a mountain in Peru. The review of literature on this symbol marked that when Venus and the sun were in conjunction with one another directly over-head, a trident symbol pointed toward a star named Sirius. The mention of the star Sirius brought to mind an ancient Mayan building at Caballito Blanco, Mexico which was constructed in the shape of an arrowhead. It pointed to the helical rising of Sirius at summer solstice.

An additional Native American archaeological site which also acknowledged the rising of this star is called the Big Horn Medicine Wheel. It is located in Wyoming.

On the other side of the Atlantic in Africa a ceremony is connected with Sirius. Von Daniken, in *Erich Von Daniken's Proof,* said that the Dogon tribe of Mali had a special bond with beings who came from Sirius and that these beings had created the tribe's ancestors. The Dogon people do a particular dance once every fifty years. Anthropologists asked them why they performed the dance so infrequently, and they replied, "Because the star Sirius has a sister star that goes around it, and it takes fifty years to make one revolution. That's why we have this ceremony only once every fifty years." Not only that, they said this planet was heavier than Sirius. Anthropologists commented in their study of existing star maps that there was no indication of a sister star revolving around Sirius. It wasn't until 1930 that Dr. Alvin Clark discovered the sister planet of Sirius, that it revolved around Sirius, and that it did, indeed, take fifty years for one revolution. Further investigation showed that this planet was more dense than Sirius. How did the "primitive" Africans know this?

The Dakota people also have an origin story connected with the stars. The story is that we came from seven stars and that we were put in the Black Hills. This origin from the seven stars is why we had only seven tribes in the beginning. It is also the reason why the number seven is sacred in our religion.

I became fascinated with this story of our star origins. Research identified the seven stars as the Pleiades. In the traditional D/Lakota history, when the Pleiades came up in the east during the fall of the year, that was a signal for the people to return to their sacred sites. Further research on the Pleiades revealed that these stars were originally seven sisters who were the daughters of Atlas and Pleione. Atlas was the oldest twin of Poseidon, the father of Atlantis.

The Creek Indians have a sacred dance called the Green Corn Dance. They take seven ears of corn from seven different fields of seven different clans. Then they perform this sacred ceremony. One of their origin stories is that they came from the stars. Was it the seven stars?

The Osage have an origin story telling that, at one time, they lived in the stars. "We were pure and noble people. Then we came onto the earth and became flesh and blood."

In a similar way, an Iroquois origin story relates that they lived in the heavens. Then they, too, came onto earth and became flesh and blood.

A Navajo origin story tells that at the beginning of this age when they emerged, they discovered a god already here. They called him Dark God. They asked him where he came from, and he said, "I came from Delyehe, the Seven Stars." [Pleiades]

Why are all these stories so similar? Is it coincidence? Or synchronicity?

In one of the origin stories of the Hopi, they say that when you can see the seven stars directly overhead at midnight, that's when the Two Horn Society sings their creation songs. The Hopi, like many other tribes, also believe that they came from the stars.

Etched crosses in stone are aligned with the rising of the seven stars in the ancient city of Teotihuacan, Mexico. On the bottom of the Aztec calendar, there are images of the creator twins--one a male and the other a female--representing the duality of every-thing in the universe. Above the heads of the twins are the seven stars of the Pleiades. The Aztecs also believed that they came from the Pleiades.

I became fascinated with this information and wanted to learn more about astronomy. I went out and purchased a zodiac dial and started to work with it. I discovered that the Pleiades follows the same path through the sky as our sun. The Pleiades is part of a larger constellation called Taurus the Bull and can be found in the shoulder hump of the bull. An ancient European story says the people believed that Taurus was a sacred white bull. When I read about a sacred white bull, I thought of the sacred white buffalo of traditional D/Lakota belief. Then I remembered a study entitled "Lakota Star Knowledge and the Black Hills," done by Sinte Gleska College in Rosebud, South Dakota in which they had identified the Pleiades as the head of a sacred white buffalo located in the stars. Further investigation identified that the stars of this sacred buffalo were related to ceremonial sites located on earth.

More research on the sacredness of the white buffalo or bull indicated that the Hindus have a sacred white bull they call Nandi. Among the Arapaho, they use the skull of a sacred buffalo in their Sun Dance.

Many other people also acknowledged the bull in a sacred manner, including the Mesopotamians and the ancient Minoans from the island of Crete. The ancient Egyptians had a bull god named Apis. In ancient Turkish ruins anthropologists found bull temples. Cro-Magnon Man in France acknowledged the bull in a sacred manner with his paintings on cave walls. Plato's writings on Atlantis stated that in the center of the metropolis of Atlantis, sacred bulls were allowed to roam free. These bulls had to do with the laws that governed the religion on Atlantis.

Becoming aware of these synchronistic stories, I grew very excited with the possibilities of man's connection to the stars through the zodiac. I decided to set my zodiac dial to the longest day of the year. I chose this day because it was the time when many Native Americans traditionally held religious ceremonies. When I positioned the dial to June 21st, I discovered that two things came up heliacally on the horizon, the Sun and Taurus the Bull. The sacred white buffalo was on the horizon at the exact time that the traditional Sun Dances were held. The traditional buffalo Sun Dance starts with the appearance of the White Buffalo Calf Woman in the east. Was the timing of the traditional Sun Dance and the rising of Taurus the Bull coincidence?

Next, I turned my zodiac dial to midnight, June 21st. As I examined the star chart on my dial, I discovered that the Milky Way was running north and south. Looking at the Milky Way, I remembered a traditional Lakota story that when you die, your spirit goes to the Milky Way. To review from the "Iyeska" chapter, when you reach there, you go south, and at the southern part of the Milky Way there is a fork where an old woman sits. She judges you by what you did on earth. If you walked the Black Road, she pushes you off and you come back to earth and are reborn. If you walked the Red Road, she allows you to return to the home of the spirits. Taking a closer look at the Milky Way, I discovered that Sagittarius was located at the southern portion of the Milky Way. In my studies of astronomy, I found that Sagittarius lies toward the direction of the center of the universe. Coincidence? Or synchronicity? Do our spirits go back from where they came?

I turned my zodiac dial to May 15th, the time when, traditionally, the vision quest was held. (One of the purposes of the vision quest was to communicate with the spirits.) I looked on the horizon that's located on the dial and discovered that, heliacally, the Pleiades was rising with the sun. The Pleiades is considered sacred by traditional D/Lakota thinkers. Isn't it interesting that the Pleiades rises with the sun at the same time the vision quest takes place?

With this question in mind, I remembered in my Biblical training that, when God challenged Job, He asked him, "Why canst thou bind the sweet influence of the Pleiades?" Was he asking, "Why can't you accept the sweet influence from Pleiades?" If so, what sweet influence is he talking about? Spiritual? I don't know.

In one of the oral history accounts of the Dakota people, it says they came from the Pleiades. How did the ancient D/Lakota know that there were seven stars in the Pleiades when you can see only six with the naked eye? Did they know because they originated there?

ORIGINS OF THE RED MAN PART II: MU

A Navajo oral history told to me by Milton Chee states that their people came from an island in the west. This island was the home of their clan mother, Changing Woman. It was also the home of all their clans. Their belief is that they came to North America by traveling on a rainbow. The psychic readings of Edgar Cayce said that there was an island in the Pacific which sank into the ocean about 28,000 B.C. Before it sank, people were warned, and they escaped to North America.

In a Hopi oral history, it is said that they came from seven islands. Some people believe these seven islands were located in the Pacific. Until recently, the Hopi conducted a ritual called the Flute Ceremony which reenacted their coming from an island.

The northwest coast of California is the traditional home of the Yurok Indians. Evan Norris, a member of the Yurok tribe, told me they had a story of an island in the Pacific named Erkager. His story related how people came from Erkager to visit his ancestors and that the island people were bad people.

Edgar Cayce declared, in the information coming from his collective unconscious, that there was an island in the Pacific called Mu. Cayce remarked that the brown race originated on the island of Mu and in South America. He also said that the red race appeared in North America and Atlantis. Both Atlantis and Mu sank beneath the oceans and all that's left of these great islands are the mountaintops.

I read a book on the island peoples of the Pacific, *Oceanic Mythology* by Roslyn Poignant. She related that when the missionaries first arrived in the Pacific islands, they asked the natives where they came from and got the reply, "We came from the underground, and we've always been here." The psychic readings of Cayce stated that Mu, also known as Lemuria, existed in the Pacific, but sank gradually into the ocean. The first cataclysm started about 50,700 B.C. The final disappearance of Mu was 28,000 B.C.

The oldest books in America belong to the ancient Mayans. Only four of the ancient books remain after the burning of the Mayan libraries by Spain's Bishop Landa in the 1600s. Richard Cavendish, editor of *Man, Myth and Magic*, an illustrated encyclopedia of the supernatural, showed a page from one of the books which tells of an island in the west.

In the Cayce readings, it is explained that the people of Mu migrated to lower California, the southwestern United States, as far north as Oregon and as far south as Peru. Remnants of the religion of the people can be found in the totem pole, explained Cayce.

He asserted that in 3000 B.C. the remaining people of the lost tribes of Israel reached America by boat from Lemuria. Reading this information triggered my memory of a passage in the *Book of Mormon*. The book of Ether (a book within the *Book of Mormon*) states that when the Jeredites first reached the Promised Land (America), "the whole face of the land northward was covered with inhabitants." Were there original inhabitants in America before the Jeredites arrived? Native American oral histories report that Native Americans originated in America.

Further research into the island of Mu uncovered the book *Understanding Mu* by Hans Stefan Santessson. Santesson wrote about a British colonel named James Churchward, who had lived in India for twenty years. While there, he visited Tibet on numerous occasions and became intrigued with the Tibetans. Upon retiring from the military, he went to Tibet and requested permission to study the old tablets located in the libraries of the ancient monasteries. In reviewing these ancient tablets, he came across a map which identified an island in the Pacific named Mu. That's the same as the Cayce readings. Coincidence? Or synchronicity? Churchward's map of this island was published in 1926.

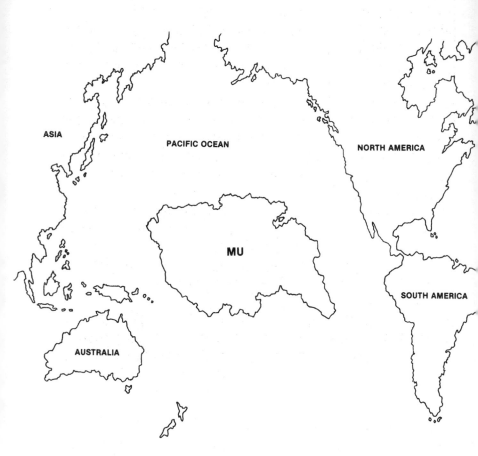

The collective unconscious of man has identified that Mu existed at this location

I reasoned that if there was an ancient continent island in the Pacific, and if people migrated east and west from it, then there should be linguistic, cultural, and architectural similarities on both sides of the Pacific.

The Yupik Eskimos of Asia have been identified as being linguistically similar to the Inupik Eskimos in America. The Manchu Tungus-speaking peoples of China have a tone value in their language that is similar linguistically to the Navajo. (In these languages, the same word said in a different tone has an entirely different meaning.) The Turkic-speaking peoples are linguistically like the Hokan-speaking peoples in the Pacific Northwest. And the Middle Eastern Aramaic-speaking people were found to be linguistically similar to the Mayans.

Churchward found the swastika symbol, which he estimated to be 70,000 years old, in the Tibetan monastery tablets. Ingrid Trayfors, a Tibetan Buddhist disciple, said the swastika is used as a religious symbol and is termed the sun symbol. I immediately remembered the Navajo religious symbol of emergence. It is called the whirling logs and is shaped like a swastika. The Hopi also use this symbol in their oral history. Their leading clans emerged from the underground, went in the four directions, and then turned right, forming a swastika symbol. The subsequent clans emerged from the underground, went in the four directions, and then turned to the left, forming a reverse swastika.

Looking at century-old photographs of beaded D/Lakota dresses, I found the swastika symbol and wondered if the D/Lakota had an ancient belief connected with this symbol, one that we had lost with the passage of time.

Archaeologists have uncovered three-legged vases in the Valley of Mexico. When the first of these was found, many thought it was the only vase of its kind until they discovered ancient pottery in China which also had only three legs.

Those who believe in the possibility of an ancient island in the Pacific state that these cultural and linguistic similarities originated in Mu.

The Great Wall exists in China, dividing China from Mongolia. It wasn't until recently that I learned of another Great Wall--in Peru. Most of it is in ruin today. Did this idea originate in the Pacific islands? Thor Hyderdaul of Kon-Tiki fame also discovered cultural similarities between Peru and the Polynesian islands.

I learned from my reading that the ancient people of Peru used to mummify their dead. This reminded me of the Egyptian mummies. In reviewing literature about the island of Mu, I discovered that the ancient Indians of the Pacific Northwest in America also mummified their dead. Cultural similarities on both sides of the Pacific again made themselves known.

The tribes of the Pacific Northwest used a totem for the thunderbird. The thunderbird totem represents purification to many tribes in North America. I recalled a related story among the Hindus that said they had a giant bird called guruda, which came to earth at the end of each age to purify the world in preparation for the new age. These two ideas, which span the Pacific Ocean, contain the same belief. How did they both come to be?

The totem pole is a universally known symbol for the people of the Pacific Northwest. In reading a book called *The Masks of God, Oriental Mythology* by Joseph Campbell, I found that carvings in ancient China had been discovered which were almost identical to the totem carvings of the Americas. In another book, *The Riddles of Three Oceans* by Alexander Kondratov, he discovered that the ancient Polynesians also used the totem pole. Kondratov discussed the possibilities of an ancient island in the Pacific and suggested it as a conceivable reason for the appearance of the totem pole on both sides of the Pacific Ocean.

A group of people known as the Ainu fishermen live in northern Japan. They are not Oriental. Many of their features are almost Caucasian in appearance. Anthropologists are still puzzled

84

as to their origins. When I saw a photograph of these Ainu people, I noticed a tremendous resemblance to the Tlingit fishermen of the Pacific Northwest. The question that entered my mind was, "Did these two groups of people originate on the island of Mu?"

In Colombia, South America giant statues with hats on the figures were found facing west toward the Pacific. On the Easter Islands, giant statues with hats on the figures almost identical to the ones in South America were facing east. What conclusions can we draw from these paradoxes? Simple coincidence?

Kondratov, investigating the old culture of the Easter Islands, found petroglyphs identical to those located in the ancient Indus Valley. He postulated that people from India had traveled to the Easter Islands and left the petroglyphs. People who believe in the island of Mu, however, say that the idea may have originated there in Mu and gone to India.

Archaeologists in India discovered that the ancient Hindus had toys with wheels on them. Kondratov pointed out that, at almost the same time in history, a toy dog with wheels was found in the Valley of Mexico. I first thought, "What in the world were Indians doing with knowledge of the wheel?" I had always been taught that we never had the wheel in the Americas. My second thought was, "Could the wheel have originated in Mu?"

In continuing my research on the islands of the Pacific, I found that many natives used a helmet design that looked like the Native American roach. Later when I was reading literature about the monks of Tibet, I discovered that they still wear a helmet of almost identical appearance to that in the Pacific islands. At this point, I was really confused! Those who believe in Atlantis felt that this design originated in Atlantis. Yet I found it to be almost universal. Churchward stated that the map he discovered which contained Atlantis and Mu showed trade routes between the two islands. The information coming from the collective unconscious of Edgar Cayce said that when these two great islands existed, much of North and South America were under water and that, in-

POLYNESIAN

PLAINS INDIAN

TIBETIAN PRIEST

Many feel that it is synchronistic that these similar head pieces appeared in North America, Polynesia (The remmnants of Mu) and in Tibet.

deed, there was trade between the two continents of Atlantis and Mu. I felt better knowing this because it helped explain the universality of the roach-looking headpiece.

The idea of trade between two ancient continent islands that no longer exist fascinated me. Contemplating this possibility, I remembered having known about a giant stone head found in ancient Mexico, on the eastern coast. Anthropologists had no idea where this figure had come from because the face had Negroid features. To me, if this part of Mexico was a trade route between Atlantis and Mu, then the appearance of a Negroid face there made sense.

The appearance of other statues in Mexico could not be explained because one was a Caucasian and the other an Oriental. These statues being discovered in a place where psychic readings

86

stated there was an ancient trade route made me wonder if the phenomenon was coincidental or synchronistic.

I studied more about the island of Mu and became aware that the aborigines of Australia were a mixture of the brown people from Mu and the black people from Africa. When I think of aborigines, the boomerang comes to mind. During my years of living among the Hopi, I discovered that they, too, had an ancient throwing stick fashioned in the shape of a boomerang. The Hopis no longer use these throwing sticks today, but they were quite common 150 years ago. Once again, I was curious about where this idea originated.

Churchward reported that the symbol of Mu was a small tree with a serpent coiled around it. The tree symbolized the island and the serpent represented water. Cayce stated, in his psychic readings, that many ideas from Mu went westward into the Eurasian country of Babylonia. Aesculapius was the ancient Greek god of medicine whose symbol was a staff with a serpent coiled around it. Some people think that the Greeks got the idea from Babylonia. Much later, in my research on the Mayan calendar, I learned that an ancient Mayan god of medicine carried a staff and had a serpent coiled around his hair. Of course, the symbol of modern medicine is a winged staff with two serpents coiled around it. Where did this idea originate?

The idea of the serpent being connected with healing interested me because I had witnessed religious ceremonies among the Hopi in which the serpent or snake was used. In studying the Hopi Snake Dance, I discovered that the snake was a messenger for the prayers of the people. After the ceremony, the serpents were taken out in the four directions and released to carry the healing prayers into Mother Earth. On the other side of the Pacific, the western side, the people of Singapore hold ancient ceremonies in which they use serpents or snakes. People in India honor the cobra in a religious manner. The serpent is a symbol for the gods, and many people give food offerings to the gods by using this symbol.

Cavendish, editor of *Man, Myth, Magic*, cited that, nowadays in southern Italy, when a statue in San Dominico is brought out and carried in the streets for religious festivals, live serpents are coiled around the statue's feet. The people use the serpent in a religious manner. Why is this idea so common around the world and where did it originate?

As I reviewed information presented in *Mysteries of the Mexican Pyramids* by Peter Tompkins, I came across the name of a geologist, William Niven, who had excavated the floor of the Valley of Mexico. Digging into the earth, he discovered a pavement nine feet below the surface. Six feet below that pavement he found a second pavement. A buried city was fourteen feet below the second pavement. The artifacts he retrieved from this city matched symbolism which Churchward saw in the ancient libraries in the monasteries of Tibet.

Churchward indicated the symbol for the creator to be the circle. He said the box symbol that was open in one corner was the symbol of the sacred four directions. The stair step symbol he identified as that of the four primary forces of the universe, and the four propeller-appearing figures meeting in the center was the symbol of the universe in movement. He saw all of these symbols not only in the monastery libraries but also in the excavation of artifacts Niven had retrieved. When I read Churchward's definitions, I recognized them as symbols of wholeness or balance. Reviewing his discussion of the open box symbol, I thought of the symbol used on ancient pottery among the Hopis. In particular, I remembered the open box symbol as the wings of an eagle.

I was delighted to observe Churchward's symbols of the open box and the stair-step woven into the design of ancient Peruvian religious tapestry I saw photographs of. In the same way, I was pleasantly surprised to view a photograph from the other side of the Pacific--a Chinese dragon painting also containing the open box symbol. (Among the ancients of China the dragon is a symbol of the gods.) Is it coincidental or synchronistic that these symbols indicate a common origin in Mu?

Churchward said the world's first religious symbol was a six-pointed star with a circle on the inside and a circle on the outside. The circle represented the creator, and the six-pointed star stood for the twelve gates to heaven (six of the points focusing outward and six focusing inward). Thinking about this symbol reminded me that Cayce declared the six-pointed star symbolized not only man's involution into matter but also his evolution back to God. Carl Jung stated, in *Man and His Symbols*, that the six-pointed star was a mandala or a symbol of wholeness. For me, more important than this research was the fact that I had seen the same symbol on Dawson No Horse's altar! (The symbols on the altars of D/Lakota holy people come from their own personal dreams.)

The symbol of the six-pointed star I also recognized as the religious symbol of the Hebrews. Further research on the Hebrews showed that they use a candlestick called a menorah that holds seven candles. The number seven is sacred to the Hebrews, as it is to the D/Lakotas. I also learned that the Hebrews held a belief in seven archangels. Why seven? Why not ten or twenty? Why seven? Could it be that it was originally a reference to the seven stars, home of the spirits?

I found that the ancient Dravidians of India had a creator symbol of a serpent with a seven-petaled flowerlike headpiece. This was fascinating to me because the creator symbol was a serpent and the number seven was evident in their religious symbol. I wondered if they had an oral history of coming from the seven stars.

As already noted, the ancient Chinese creator symbol was the dragon. The Chinese believed that the dragon came from the heavens. The D/Lakota story that we came from the heavens (in particular the Pleiades) implies a similar origin.

One day I was giving a lecture on the origins of the D/Lakota being in the Pleiades or the seven stars. After the lecture, a man from the audience came up to me and said, "We have that same story in our oral history." I asked him where he was from and he said he was an Inca Indian from Peru.

In Peru on the Nazca Plains a giant thunderbird is carved into the floor of the valley. Tony Morrison, in *Pathways to the Gods-- The Mystery of the Andes Lines*, "...calls the...Thunderbird, 'The Plaza of the Pleiades' because it is oriented directly to the rising of the Pleiades at the estimated time of construction."

Research done by Lee J. Elders and Thomas K. Welch on earth structures connected to the Pleiades showed that within the Great Pyramid of Cheops at Giza, the King's Chamber was built according to a mathematical design that was proportional to the length of time it takes our sun to rotate once around the Pleiades. The idea that the King's Chamber represents the Pleiades excited me because I had read in the Cayce material that this pyramid was used as a temple of initiation for the ancients. When a person fasted there, he was initiated by the spirits or God.

Does mankind have an origin connection with the Pleiades? Is all of this information interwoven?

TAKU WAKAN SKAN SKAN: SOMETHING HOLY MOVING

Traditionally, the D/Lakota believed that your spirit never died. When the body died, it was placed, in the traditional manner, on a scaffold for four seasons, this length of time allowing the spirit to journey onward. At the end of the four seasons, what was left of the body was taken down and hidden or buried.

In the early 1900s, a man by the name of George Sword acted as interpreter to James Walker, a government doctor. Walker was interested in gathering information about traditional D/Lakota religious thought. Sword recorded information given to him by the holy man, Finger, who stated that "skan" was the sky, as well as a spirit that was everywhere, giving life to everything that moves. Finger's interpretation of "Taku skan skan" was "what moves moves" or "that which gives motion to everything that moves." Apparently, he believed that this was a force or energy. I have chosen to call this energy taku wakan skan skan, "something holy moving."

In my investigation to find corresponding evidence which supports Native American traditional philosophy and thought, I decided to search out a psychic interpretation of energy. Gladys Moore, whose spirit guide is Samuel, commented in *Forgotten Knowledge*:

Infinite energy, that is the creator of all things, is the beginning energy that is, and always was, and will always be God. A beginning of life in humans is a part of this infinite energy of God's, and is all love, the most powerful force in your dimension of life. This energy, becoming a life, was a plan of God to expand the force of love. This is why, as a part of God's infinite energy, you are all Sons of God.

I understand this to mean that the spirit of God is energy that never dies and that this energy has entered the body of all people.

According to psychic information transmitted by Edgar Cayce, God's energy is many individual parts, yet it is all one. Cayce said that this energy entered human bodies in five different locations at the same time: the white race in the Caucasus and the Carpathian Moun tains; the red race in North America and Atlantis; the yellow race in Mongolia; the black race in the Sudan and upper West Africa; and the brown race in South America and Mu. I wanted to see what modern physics had to say about energy. "Energy is equal to mass times the speed of light squared" is the famous equation of how Einstein defined energy. He received this information through a vision. One day he was resting on top of a hill, and he imagined himself traveling to the sun and returning. When he returned, he realized he had traveled in a curved line. This visionary information came to him via the right hemispheric process. He needed to put it into a scientific equation that would lend itself to a more left hemispheric function. He developed his theory of relativity based on the equation, which identified light as traveling in a curved line. In my own mind, I felt that if one extends continuously the curve in which light travels, it becomes a circle. In my way of thinking, Einstein's theory has shown modern man that all things move in circles, thus giving credence to the concept of wholeness.

In *The Dancing Wu Li Masters*, Gary Zukav remarked: "What Einstein had to say about space and time is that there is no such thing as space *and* time; there is only space-time. Space-time is a continuum." I started to develop a space-time continuum model based on research which I applied to the model. This model was a drawing of a cube, identified by its height, width, and depth. The cube is a three-dimensional figure. Anyone looking at it would establish a fourth dimension. If you could view yourself seeing that three- dimensional figure, you would establish a fifth dimension.

Contemplating this concept, I recalled what I had read about astral projection. Cayce reported that in astral projection, a per

92

son's spirit is able to leave the body. This made me think, "Is the fifth dimension the place that we call the spirit world?"

Once again, in *The Dancing Wu Li Masters*, Zukav said, If we could view our reality in a four-dimensional way, we would see that everything that now seems to unfold before us with the passing of time, already exists *in toto*, painted, as it were, on the fabric of space-time. We would see all, the past, the present, and the future with one glance.

My interpretation is that if a person is able to transcend himself into the fifth dimension, he would be able to see everything. Rationalizing this concept, I immediately remembered Cayce saying that when you make contact with the collective unconscious, everything that was or will be is now. Is it coincidental or synchronistic that the fifth dimension and the collective unconscious are the same?

Fritjof Capra remarked, in his book *The Tao of Physics*, that a technique for making contact with the collective unconscious was through meditation. One of the methods that the D/Lakota people use to make contact with the collective unconscious is the sacred pipe ceremony.

The collective unconscious, as previously discussed, is the lower part of the mind. My continuing studies about the mind led me to information on the brain. Scientists now estimate that there are 100 billion cells in our brain. It is felt that each cell functions as a hologram. I began to delve into the area of holography. I found that a hologram is a projection of an image in mid-air without the aid of a screen. This projected image has a three-dimensional effect, and a person can walk completely around it without disturbing it. Holography is a special system of projection which uses a series of mirrors placed at different angles that allow the image to be projected at a single point.

Once when I was giving a presentation on this subject at the University of Colorado in Denver, one of the audience members approached me afterward and asked me if I had ever seen a hologram. I hadn't. He described to me a holographic device he had seen demonstrated at Martin-Marietta in Denver. He declared that the holographic image projected was, in fact, projected in mid-air without the aid of a screen.

Intrigued with the concept, I continued my reading in that area. It seems that holography is forcing modern man to re-evaluate his visual traditions in order to understand it. At the most basic level, when you view a hologram, you don't look *at* it; rather, you look *into* it.

Returning to my three-dimensional cube, I decided to shade the vertical wall. When a person sees this cube, he is able to place the shaded wall at the back of the cube or, in his own mind, to make the shaded wall appear at the front of the cube. In *The Holography Book*, Jeff Berner commented, "A hologram can be viewed inside out and backwards (pseudoscopically) just by turning it back to front." (The shaded wall of the cube, as already mentioned, can be placed in either position--in the same manner as looking at a hologram--by the mind of the viewer.) "This unique perspective is like being inside the imagery looking out to where the viewer would normally be," continued Berner.

Neuropsychologists and holographers jointly concur that our brain works holographically. The human brain is the only organ that can see itself seeing.

"Are we holographic reflections of the universe?" is a question that came up among holographers. The possibilities of this question greatly fascinated me because I saw implications as to how holography could be part of the traditional ceremonies. An example of this is in the construction and use of the kiva. To review, a kiva is a circular structure built below ground level, the doorway an opening in the roof.

A few years ago my present wife Dorothy and I witnessed a ceremonial dance at one of the Rio Grande pueblos in New Mexico. It was her first time at this type of dance, and she asked me many questions. I was able to answer a few, but not the vast majority.

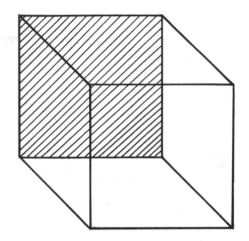

Imagine the shaded wall to be in front of the cube, or in the rear of the cube. This pseudoscopic technique is used by the Native American when he enters the sweat lodge or the Kiva.

This made me curious. That night I had a dream in which the kiva and a model of the psyche appeared as the same. The top of the kiva represented the ego. When you entered the kiva, you were entering the collective unconscious part of the mind. The dancers who emerged from the kiva represented archetypal figures from the collective unconscious. When I woke up, I remembered the dream and felt very happy, for now I knew the esoteric meaning behind the dancers performing in the plaza. I realized that when a Hopi person enters the kiva in a traditional manner, he is no longer himself; he is part of the kachina world.

A second example is found in the sweat lodge. I learned, through personal experience, that when you enter the sacred sweat lodge, no longer are you a two-legged man; you are now one with the spirit world. D/Lakota prayers end with, "Mitakuye Oyasin," which means, "We are all related." Everything in the universe is related. This frame of mind allowed me to be able to look out where the viewer would normally be. My experience made me believe this must be how a person would feel when he was in the kiva. Is this experience the answer that the holographers sought for the question of our being holographic reflections of the universe? If so, is this realization a coincidental event? Or a synchronistic one?

Reflecting on the term, "Mitakuye Oyasin," I remembered reading in *The Tao of Physics* that Capra had said, "The basic oneness of the universe is not only the central characteristic of the mystical experience, but is also one of the most important revelations of modern physics." I questioned, "If everything in the universe is related, how is it related?"

Knowledge about the galaxies came through as I probed more deeply into the mysteries of the universe. I became aware that there are 100 billion galaxies in our universe. Our galaxy, the Milky Way, is in a spiral shape, and our solar system is located approximately at the tip of one of the curves of the spiral. Scientists now estimate the possibility of life from other parts of the universe to be very likely. Are UFOs the life from other parts of the universe that scientists believe may exist?

I became interested in UFO studies and started to read books containing UFO material. Dr. Jung, in *Memories, Dreams, Reflections*, wrote about how UFOs relate to the collective unconscious. He stated that modern man used to think of UFOs as their own projections, but now realizes he himself is the projection of the UFOs. But Jung wanted to know who was at the controls in the UFOs. Writing in *Flying Saucers*, he believed that, "UFOs come from the unconscious background, which always expresses itself in numinous ideas and images." It's one thing to study the psychology of UFOs but quite another thing to actually see them.

KIVA

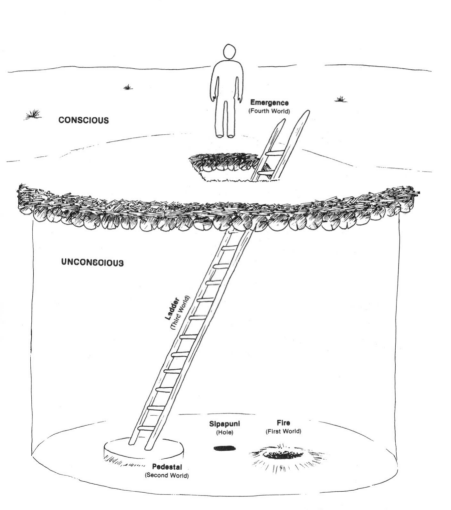

CONSCIOUS

Emergence
(Fourth World)

UNCONSCIOUS

Ladder
(Third World)

Sipapuni
(Hole)

Fire
(First World)

Pedestal
(Second World)

Dr. Ross's dream equated the inside of a Kiva with the unconscious
part of the psyche

I used to patronize a bookstore on the west side of Denver. One day the owner called me and said she'd just gotten in a new book on UFOs and thought I might be interested because she knew of my research in this area. I quickly went and got the book. I was completely surprised at the title: *UFO...Contact from the Pleiades* by Lee J. Elders and Thomas K. Welch. It is a well-documented account of a man named Eduard "Billy" Meier, a farmer in Switzerland, who made contact with UFO cosmonauts. One day he had a compelling urge to get up and walk out to his pasture lands. When he got there, three UFO cosmonauts met him and communicated with him through mental telepathy. Semjase, the female cosmonaut leader, told Meier on February 8, 1975:

We, too, are still far removed from perfection and have to evolve constantly, just like yourselves. We are neither superior nor super-human, nor are we missionaries...we feel duty bound to the citizens of Earth, because our forefathers were your forefathers...

When I read this, I remembered the D/Lakota oral story that we came from seven stars, we were placed in the Black Hills, and this is why we had seven tribes. The Ojibway, too, have an oral story that says there were beings who came from seven stars. They married some of the Ojibway women. As I thought about the remarks of the cosmonaut, I wondered if she was talking about the forefathers as physical beings or as spiritual beings. Semjase also said:

Man should know that the God (force) is quite simply that of creation, and that man also, either coming from the higher spiritual spheres or being elevated to those spheres after numerous terrestrial lives, is subject to creation and respectively complimentary to it.

These words put me in mind of the traditional D/Lakota view that when someone kills out of anger, he's walking the Black Road, and that guarantees his spirit being reborn into a new body for further growth and expansion. This is why it is more honorable to touch one's enemy than to kill him.

Semjase continued:

The higher he [man] soars, the greater becomes his power. However, one can never identify God separately from the creation because God itself is a part of it, with all the rest of the "gods" who co-exist with it in various states of being, stages of instant celestial substance which are perfectly adapted to them.

Once again a piece of traditional D/Lakota philosophy came to me. Royal Hassrick, in *The Sioux*, said:

There was, and is, and will be Wakan Tanka, the Great Mystery. He is one yet many. He is the Chief God, the Great Spirit, the Creator, and the Executive. He is the Gods both Superior and Associate and He is the Gods-Kindred, both the Subordinate and the Gods-like. He is the good and evil gods, the visible and invisible, the physical and immaterial, for He is all

Pondering the similarity in these statements, once again I wondered, "Is this coincidence? Or is it synchronicity?"

As I continued reading in the *UFO...Contact from the Pleiades*, I learned that the UFO cosmonauts told Billy Meier that they live on a planet named Erra, and that this planet is within the constellation of the Pleiades. They said it only takes them seven hours in earth time to get here. I thought to myself, "How in the world do they get here so fast?" The Pleiades is 500 light years away; if they traveled at the speed of light, it would take them 500 years. Yet they get here in seven hours. How do they travel? Thought projection?

Semjase said, "By creative thinking man acquires knowledge and wisdom and a sense of unlimited strength which unbinds him from the limitations of convention and dogma." In the research I've done on the brain, I know that creative thinking is right-brain thinking and currently, modern man is left-brain-dominant. Is this the reason for modern man's adherence to "convention and dogma"?

The Pleiadian cosmonauts told Billy Meier that they are not the only intelligent life in the universe. At last count, there were 108 other civilizations like theirs within the universe, and they are 3000 years in advance of ours.

The author of *UFO...Contact from the Pleiades* said:

However, the Pleiadians and other highly evolved 'Beings of Light' do not see Earth humanity obtaining control of their destiny...They warned Meier that, in their opinion, we terrestrials were not capable of changing mass consciousness, that we are an insane society rushing headlong to our own destruction, that we were not only content with exterminating each other, but we now are bent on destroying all forms of life on this planet as well as the critical life support systems. At this stage of our evolution they and other extraterrestrial life forms consider us an experiment, and they are deeply saddened, for they consider us their younger brothers, separated only by a different space and time.

I recalled that in our oral history, previous ages are referred to as a time when we had technology. We misued it, and mankind destroyed himself. Is that when the traditional Native Americans developed the philosophy of respect for Mother Earth and all living things on her? I wondered, "Is the destruction of previous ages through misuse of technology the reason why the traditional people at Taos Pueblo don't have electricity and modern plumbing?" The traditional people in Walpi Village on the Hopi Reservation have no electricity or modern conveniences for that reason.

The Mandan Tribe in North Dakota had a traditional ceremony called Okeepa where a holy man came out into the village center and shouted, "I am the last man!" He cried out this phrase until all the people gathered around, and he told them he had just come from a place that had been destroyed by a great flood. He was the only survivor, the last man. He asked the people to go into their homes and bring out a modern implement. They put them in a pile and burned them as a gesture of refusing modern technology.

According to Hopi tradition, misuse of technology is what brought about the flood that destroyed the last age. In the psychic readings of Edgar Cayce, too, it was pointed out that previous ages were destroyed through misuse of technology and that the great flood of which the Bible speaks happened 28,000 years ago. As recorded in his book *The Stones of Atlantis*, David Zink hired a psychic named Carol Huffstickler to locate the sunken city off the shores of the Bimini Islands. When she did a reading on the sunken city, she said it was part of Atlantis and that it was built 28,000 years ago. It was not built with tools but with the aid of Beings of Light who had come from the Pleiades. She went on to say that these Beings of Light who had appeared 28,000 years ago came not just to help build the city but also to help mankind correct the imbalance in brain hemisphericy. Apparently, 28,000 years ago, which Cayce said was the end of the last age, mankind was left-brain dominant. Now, the prophecy is that we are approaching the end of this age, and mankind is out of balance again. "We live in a 'left-brain' society, and nowhere is this more emphasized than in the schools," remarked Alfred W. Munzert in *Test Your IQ*.

When I learned about the Beings of Light coming from the Pleiades 28,000 years ago to restore the balance, I asked myself, "Was this one of the functions of the UFO cosmonauts coming from the Pleiades today?"

The constellation of the Pleiades has surfaced many times in my life. I remember when I was working at the Community College in Denver, several students from the Middle East would stop by my office to visit. I knew, by the questions they asked, that they were interested in Native American philosophy and thought. As they questioned me about these traditional things, I could see they were mentally comparing it with their own belief systems. I asked, then, if they had stories that related to some of the ones I'd told them. They had a story in the Koran which included the seven stars or the Pleiades.

101

The Koran says that the angel Gabriel came from the Pleiades to teach Mohammed all the laws by which mankind should live. I wondered, "Was Gabriel a Pleiadian cosmonaut?"

In D/Lakota oral history, a spiritual woman came to us and brought us the sacred pipe that was to be used in the seven sacred rites, laws by which we should live. When she came, she carried the pipe in her left hand, and in her right hand was a stone that had seven circles etched on it. Where did she come from? Why did she have seven circles on the stone in her right hand? What intrigued me at this point was that Semjase, the leader of the Pleiadian cosmonauts who spoke to Billy Meier was a female.

In 1981 my twin daughters Dana and Dawn and their girlfriend Melinda went to their first sweat lodge ceremony, during which a woman's beautiful voice was heard singing sweat lodge songs. When they emerged from the lodge, the twins' mother Dorothy said to them, "I didn't know you girls knew the songs."

"We don't," they replied, "it must've been Melinda." Melinda said, "It wasn't me singing the songs."

Everyone looked at each other, startled. My first thought was that it may have been my wife's mother's spirit. My second thought was that it was the White Buffalo Calf Woman. I went to Dawson No Horse and told him of the experience, asking him who he thought it was. He said, "It might have been the White Buffalo Calf Woman. She is back."

Later I learned that, in that same summer, as recorded in a July 1987 issue of *Newsweek*, the Virgin Mary had appeared in a vision to six children in Medjugorje, Yugoslavia. I wondered if there was a link in some way between these two women. Were their appearances coincidental or synchronistic?

The White Buffalo Calf Woman told the D/Lakota people that they should use the pipe in the seven sacred rites. These rites are the sweat lodge, crying for a vision, the Sun Dance, the White Buffalo Maiden, Adoption, Keeping of the Soul, and Throwing of the Ball.

102

All of the ceremonies are used in many ways, but each is most noted for the following: the sweat lodge is a purification ceremony, both physically and spiritually. Crying for a vision, a vision quest, is a period of meditation with fasting. A thanksgiving ceremony, the Sun Dance is done to give thanks to Father Sun for all he has provided Mother Earth. A puberty ceremony for young girls is the purpose of the White Buffalo Maiden ceremony. The adoption ceremony is used to adopt more children, more parents, more brothers, more sisters. It is a recognition of the extended family. Keeping of the soul was usually done for youngsters who died and did not have time to grow and expand in this life. The parents kept the soul for one year, during which time they prayed for the soul to gain growth and expansion. Then the soul was released to return to the spirit world. The throwing of the ball ceremony I knew very little about when I first read about the White Buffalo Calf Woman and this ceremony. I began to study it.

The ceremony is based on a dream that Standing Buffalo had. The following narration of this ceremony was given by Black Elk to Joseph Epes Brown. The playing field is marked off in four quarters, each of the four directions represented. A little girl who held a sacred ball in her hand stood at the center of the field. The ball was colored red, and it had two blue strips painted on it, crossing each other at right angles to form the four directions. Buffalo people stood at each of the four directions on the playing field. The little girl threw the ball high into the air to the west. As it descended upon the buffalo people, all of a sudden they turned into two-legged people. They caught the ball and returned it to the girl in the center. She threw the ball to the north. The same sequence was repeated. Then she threw the ball to the east and then to the south, and each time the sequence of the buffalo turning into two-leggeds and returning the ball to her occurred. The fifth time, she threw the ball straight up in the air. As the ball descended upon the people, they turned back into buffalo and could not catch it.

103

Black Elk said that this game represented man's life. The playing field stood for the universe; the center of the playing field represented Wakan Tanka or God. The ball also represented Wakan Tanka. The buffalo had no hands and couldn't catch the ball, a representation of ignorance or walking the Black Road.

In *The Sacred Pipe* Joseph Epes Brown recorded Black Elk's words:

"I, Black Elk, should now explain to you several things that you may not understand about this holy rite. First, it is a little girl, and not an older person, who stands at the center and who throws the ball. This is as it should be, for just as *Wakan-Tanka* is eternally youthful and pure, so is this little one who has just come from *Wakan-Tanka*, pure and without any darkness. Just as the ball is thrown from the center to the four quarters, so *Wakan-Tanka* is at every direction and is everywhere in the world; and as the ball descends upon the people, so does His power, which is only received by a very few people, especially in these last days.

"You have seen that the four-legged buffalo people were not able to play this game with the ball, and so they gave it to the two-leggeds. This is very true because, as I have said before, of all the created things or beings of the universe, it is the two-legged men alone who, if they purify and humiliate themselves, may become one with--or may know--*Wakan-Tanka*.

"At this sad time today among our people we are scrambling for the ball, and some are not even trying to catch it, which makes me cry when I think of it. But soon I know it will be caught, for the end is rapidly approaching, and then it will be returned to the center, and our people will be with it. It is my prayer that this be so, and it is in order to aid in this 'recovery of the ball,' that I have wished to make this book."

Just before Black Elk's death in the early 1950s, he prophesied that soon someone would catch the ball (become one with Wakan Tanka). In the process of catching it, that person would return it to the center of the playing field (center of the universe). This prophecy reminded me of how Dawson No Horse received his power.

He told me that in 1974, while he was still an Episcopal priest, he was drawn to attend the Sun Dance. While observing it, he saw a person standing in the center by the tree. He asked someone standing next to him, "Who is that standing out there?" The man replied, "I don't see anybody."

Wanting an explanation for his vision, Dawson went to Frank Fools Crow, an Oglala holy man. Frank immediately recognized what was happening and told Dawson to fast on the hill for four days and four nights. Dawson said that the first three days, nothing happened--he was only aware of his hunger, his thirst, and insects eating at him. On the fourth day, a thunderstorm appeared and a bolt of lightning came out of the storm and struck right beside him. The man he had seen at his vision in the Sun Dance stood where the lightning had struck. This man's name was Canupa Gluha Mani (Walks with the Pipe).

After Dawson came down from the hill, Fools Crow started teaching him yuwipi songs and how to conduct the ceremony because he knew that Dawson was supposed to become a yuwipi man. Canupa Gluha Mani was Dawson's main spirit helper in the yuwipi ceremony.

For seven years Dawson held ceremonies in which hundreds of people were healed. He carried the ball or walked with God for seven years. Then he told his family, "They're calling me on the other side. It's time for me to go."

His family said, "Don't talk like that."

"I know that a lot of these things I have done you have a hard time believing," he replied, "but I tell you now that it's time for me to go." And he planned his own funeral. He said all people were welcome to attend, no matter what religion, no matter what race. On January 28, 1982, the body of Dawson No Horse died. I believe his spirit returned to the center of the universe.

Black Elk's explanation of the seventh rite and the information coming from the collective unconscious of Edgar Cayce were almost the same. Cayce said that a person is reincarnated again and again until he becomes whole. Each incarnation is an opportunity for the individual to grow and expand. Cayce stated that when one has fulfilled his karmic debts (sins committed in this life and previous lives), then that individual becomes one with God and his will conforms with the will of the Creator, his earthly cycles are finished, and his soul may return to the center of the universe. Is this what happened to Dawson? Did he become whole or one with everything? Is Dawson the person who fulfilled Black Elk's prophecy?

THE FLOWERING TREE

This chapter is a comparison between psychic and Native American healing. One of the reasons I selected the title, "The Flowering Tree" is because, in Black Elk's great vision, that is what he saw. The spirits took him to the center of the universe where there was a flowering tree. My understanding of the flowering tree in Black Elk's vision is that it is a symbol of Wakan Tanka or God. I say this because the sacred tree in the center of the Sun Dance is a symbol of God, and the Sun Dance circle represents the universe.

The concept of a tree being sacred brought back memories of my Christian teachings about the sacred evergreen tree that stands for everlasting life. Just as this tree is always green, one's spirit never dies.

In Taos Pueblo on San Geronimo Day, the people place a sacred tree in the middle of the plaza, and it represents the center of the universe. Offerings to God are placed at the top of this pole. The sacred clowns then climb it to accept the offerings. Frank Waters, in his book *Masked Gods: Pueblo and Navajo Ceremonialism,* stated that many tribes had a pole climbing ritual. Thinking about the many different peoples who hold this similar belief, I remembered a statement by Carl Jung, that the spiritual problem of modern man is that we're looking outside for salvation, when we should be looking inside. "This sacred tree that we have must also be inside," I thought.

I searched for evidence of a sacred tree within and found one of the Hindu beliefs to be that a sacred tree is within each individual, the tree consisting of seven vibratory centers, also known as chakras. Each of the invisible chakras is connected to the spinal column. If they were visible, according to the Hindus, they would look like a flower blossom.

I was reminded of the traditional Hopi belief, that there are vibratory centers in the human body. To review from "Original

107

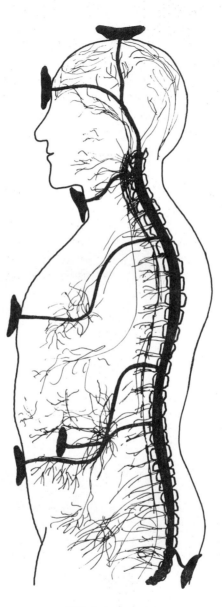

THE FLOWERING TREE

The chakra system is activated by different vibrations of light (color)

Teachings of the Red Man," these centers are located at the crown of the head, the forehead, the throat, the heart, and the solar plexus. Psychic readings of Edgar Cayce indicated that these seven vibratory centers are connected to the endocrine glands. Cayce also said that the seven angels, the seven golden candlesticks, the seven plagues that are mentioned in the first chapter of Revelation in the Bible are nothing more than symbols for the seven chakras or spiritual centers of the body.

I did not know what the endocrine glands were. I found, upon reading about this system, that they were a classification of glands including the pituitary, the pineal, the thyroid, the thymus, the adrenals, the lyden, and the gonads. Cayce said that each of the energy centers was activated by a different vibration of light. Red activates the gonads; orange, the lyden; yellow, the adrenals; green, the thymus; blue, the thyroid; indigo, the pineal; and violet, the pituitary. When the vibration of light activates a certain center, that center, in turn, activates an endocrine gland. According to *The Rainbow Book* edited by F. Lanier Graham, each of the vibratory colors also has certain properties, some of those char acteristics being: red for birth, beginning, sex; orange for power, glory, the sun; yellow for intellect, joy, sensation; green for growth, healing, vegetation; blue for spirit, heaven, psychic ability; indigo for intuition, seeking, spirituality; and violet for transition, separation, advanced spirituality.

Reading how colors influence chakra characteristics within the body caused me to recall the sacred colors of the four directions that we have in D/Lakota religion. For example, in the Sun Dance, I witnessed one of the sacred colors being used for healing. Almost all tribes, in fact, use sacred colors in their religions.

I found that the Mayan Indians used black for the west, white for the north, red for the east, and yellow for the south. These colors and their relationship to the directions were the same as what Black Elk had received in his vision. I wondered if all these similarities were coincidental or synchronistic.

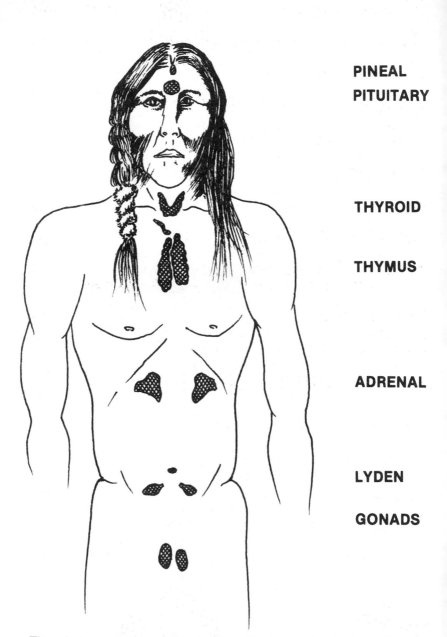

PINEAL
PITUITARY

THYROID

THYMUS

ADRENAL

LYDEN

GONADS

The chakra or vibatory centers enable the endocrine glands to function

A chart in *The Rainbow Book* identified sound vibrations, in addition to color, as activating the chakras. I was curious about whether the sounds emitted by the instruments used in Native American healing ceremonies correlate with the chakras that deal specifically with healing. (My research indicated that the four highest chakras were associated with healing.)

The first instrument I checked was the drum because all healing ceremonies utilize the drum. At this point, I was working at the Community College in Denver, and I took a drum, as well as a rattle and a whistle, to the electronics laboratory. The technicians used a meter which measured sound frequency. To my amazement, the frequencies produced by all three instruments were the same as those that correlate with the highest four chakras.

In researching spiritual healing, I learned it is believed that all healing comes from our own inner spirit and that God is the source of that healing. The flowering tree is within as well as without.

The endocrine system has a role in spiritual healing. A monthly publication of the Association for Research and Enlightenment, Inc., "Covenant," Vol. 2, No. 2, Lesson XIV: Holistic Healing, stated:

The system within our bodies which is most capable of bringing about the proper balance of all the atoms in the body is the endocrine system. When quickened, attuned and aligned, and working in accord one with another under the direction of the higher centers (especially the pituitary), these glands may send out hormonal messages to all the cells of the body, awakening and instructing them in their proper functioning.

The four glands used in healing are the pineal, located in the middle of the forehead; the pituitary in the center of the brain; the thyroid at the throat area; and the thymus in the upper chest.

Another technique used in spiritual healing is the laying on of hands. From the "Covenant" publication cited above: The laying on of hands, which through the centuries has been fraught with much misunderstanding, is highly recommended by the [Cayce] readings. It need not necessarily be given by one who has the reputation of being a healer.

My immediate association was with the laying on of hands as used in the Sun Dance. I personally know people who have been healed at the Sun Dance.

As described in the "Original Teachings of the Red Man" chapter, sacred clowns are a part of many tribal traditions. One of their functions is to provide amusement and laughter, in the midst of serious ceremonies, to help the people be more balanced and whole. Additionally, the laughter itself can be healing for those involved. In fact, current research, as cited by Norman Cousins in *Anatomy of an Illness as Perceived by the Patient,* has reported the therapeutic effects of laughter as an aid in healing a sick person.

The psychic readings of Edgar Cayce stated that any illness can be healed if the person aligns his will to the will of the spirit within. When a person achieves this alignment, he then becomes whole and at one with everything around him. This idea is much like a passage from the Bible where, after Jesus had healed a woman, he told her, "Daughter, thy faith hath made thee whole: go in peace, and be whole of thy plague."

I questioned, "Why are all these examples of healing so similar? What overall principle is at work here?

Another passage from the Bible stated, "The kingdom of God cometh not with observation: ...for, behold, the kingdom of God is within you." Dr. Jung believed that the archetype of the Supreme Being exists within the collective unconscious.

Wanting to learn more about the activities of the unconscious mind, I went to a hypnotist while I was living in Denver. He said that when he works with a client, he uses four laws of the mind. I could see how they related to traditional Native American philosophy and thought. The first law is: "The mind has the ability to be directed toward a field of concentrated attention." Remember this sentence?

> FINISHED FILES ARE THE RE-
> SULT OF YEARS OF SCIENTIF-
> IC STUDY COMBINED WITH THE
> EXPERIENCE OF MANY YEARS.

You were told to count the number of "f"s. The majority of people can see only three because they associate the symbol with the sound of "f."

The second law is: "The mind will focus itself in reversed effort [reverse psychology]." Previously, I had talked about people who came to be out of balance spiritually. A way that the traditional D/Lakota culture helped maintain the balance was through use of the "heyoka." The heyoka did everything backwards on purpose. He purposely did everything wrong. Yet he was also "wicasa wakan," a holy man, with the powers to heal.

The third law is: "The mind can be directed toward dominant desire." This law reinforced my belief in the sacred pipe. When you use the pipe to request information, a feather is tied on the stem at the place where it meets the bow.

The fourth law is: "The mind has the ability to achieve by repetition with belief." Remember how I explained earlier about the traditional D/Lakota religious custom of making many, many tobacco ties? You take your ties into a ceremony as an offering and receive an answer to your prayers.

In reviewing this fourth law, I was reminded of Hindu holy men who use prayer beads. They say their prayers repeatedly while counting the beads. I once saw a picture of an Indian fakir (holy man) lying on a bed of nails counting his prayer beads. It made me wonder if, by his using the prayer beads, he was able to accomplish this feat.

The practice of using prayer beads brought to mind a story I read in one of the major news magazines. An army chaplain was taken prisoner during the Korean War. To help pass the time, he used his rosary when he said his prayers. A voice spoke to him in the darkness of his cell, responding to his repeated prayers. All of these uses of repetitious prayer that achieve results was a gratifying discovery for me. And the haunting question again came up: "Was this discovery coincidental or synchronistic?" These continual disclosures--which showed how all things are related--reminded me of the words the D/Lakota use when they end their prayers. The words are "Mitakuye oyasin." The literal interpretation is, "All my relations." The esoteric meaning is, "We are all related." I know that modern physics has a similar concept, in that physicists recognize a oneness in the universe.

But I did not know that in ancient Egypt, there was a god of unity, a god of oneness whose name was Amon. The Hebrews had lived in Egypt for over 1000 years. When they returned to their homeland, they were using the word, "Amen" to end their prayers. I was curious about a possible connection. Once when I presented this lecture, a rabbi in the audience said he felt that the Egyptians had gotten the word similarity from the Hebrews.

The concept that we are all related is one of the basic philosophies of D/Lakota religion. In a traditional manner, prayers were said for the animal before the hunter even went on a hunt. A thanksgiving ceremony was held after a successful hunt. I was pleasantly surprised when I learned from Kathleen Bour's article "Love All God's Creatures" that, "Mahatma Gandhi said that one could determine the morals of a nation by the way it treats its animals."

Modern physics shows a relationship among all things in the universe. Edgar Cayce's psychic readings stated that sun spots were created by negative energy produced by human brain waves. He commented that the whole planet is surrounded with this negative energy because there are so many bad thoughts. That made me think of William Herrmann, the man who was abducted by a UFO. The cosmonauts told him it was very difficult for them to come to Planet Earth. The planet has "aura stench," according to

114

UFO information received by Ruth Montgomery, which she wrote about in *Strangers Among Us: Enlightened Beings from a World to Come.* The negative energy affects the sun, which repels it, producing sun spots. The sun spot effect on Planet Earth is weather changes, the appearance of unknown diseases, earthquakes, volcanoes, and depletion of the ozone layer.

If the psychic readings about the effect of the negative energy on our solar system are true, then, indeed, we *are* all related. Traditional philosophy of American Indians stated that the sun is our father, and the earth is our mother. Many tribes have religious ceremonies in which they send good energy to the sun. In Taos Pueblo on San Geronimo Day, the people participate in religious races, which are actually prayers that send good energy to the sun. The ancient Cherokees performed a sunrise ceremony in which they prayed to help the sun on its journey because they believed it had to break free from the earth. In the D/Lakota Sun Dance, there is a time when the dancers raise their hands, giving thanks to the sun; then they drop their arms toward the earth and back to themselves, thus creating a cycle of good energy. In the traditional D/Lakota way of thinking, all things go in cycles; for example, if you wish for good health in your life, you pray for others to receive good health.

I was pleasantly surprised while watching the film "Gandhi" at a situation where a Hindu man approached Gandhi and reported that the Moslems had killed his son. He, in turn, had killed a Moslem youth. Gandhi told him if he wanted to rid himself of this negative karma, he needed to find an orphaned Moslem boy the same age as his son was and raise him as his own. But he also needed to raise this boy as a Moslem.

Ella Deloria, in her book *Speaking of Indians,* reported that this idea of replacing a murdered child with a member of the murderer's family to be raised as your own child was an ancient D/Lakota custom.

115

This traditional philosophy is also expressed in the Sun Dance when the dancers suffer so that the people may live. Many things happen at the Sun Dance. It is not only healing for the earth, but for participants as well as observers. I remember one year I had made a pledge to give myself to Wakan Tanka. I chose to do this by pulling seven buffalo skulls. The skin on the back is pinched and an incision made for the cherry-wood skewer to go through. A rope is tied to the skewer, and the skulls are attached to the other end of the rope. The individual, in a very sacred manner, drags the skulls until the skin breaks free. While I dragged the skulls, I had a vision of Christ.

I did not tell anybody about this for two years because I did not understand what Christ was doing in the Sun Dance. I was comforted with the fact, though, that the Bible says, "Wherever two or three are gathered together in my name, there I am in the midst of them."

Traditional D/Lakota people believe in spirits. These spirits are invisible. Sometimes they show themselves in the clouds or in a vision or in a dream. Almost all traditional Native Americans had a belief in spirits. The Hopi called their spirits kachina. They felt that the kachina was an earthly representation of invisible spirits.

Did the ancient Christians believe in spirits? They had figures with wings, and they called them angels. The word angel comes from the Greek language and means spirit.

The psychic readings of Edgar Cayce stated that all matter contains spirit and that spirits have electrical properties.

Ruth Montgomery, in *Strangers Among Us: Enlightened Beings from a World to Come,* declared that spirits exist in groups. She said there are sixty groups serving humanity and that each of these sixty has a group mind. Group mind can be described as all of the spirits in one group having identical thought patterns. Montgomery related, "Group Mind is a fifth-dimension phenomenon." I understood this to mean that the spirits exist in the fifth dimension. This is the answer I was looking for when I questioned whether the fifth dimension was the place we call the spirit world.

People are most receptive to the group mind energy when they are in the alpha brain wave state, remarked Montgomery. She continued, "This is a relaxed, passive state in which you are scarcely aware of that which flows into and out of the mind, and is most often achieved during meditation..." Brain waves indicate different states of consciousness: delta, a deep sleep, the higher states of awareness; alpha, a passive, blank state; and beta, the thinking, active state. Alpha is in the center between beta and delta. The holy men communicate with the spirits, and a philosophy of the holy people is to walk the Red Road. The Red Road is in the center between pairs of opposites. Does the traditional D/Lakota concept of the Red Road equate to scientifically-produced alpha waves?

Ruth Montgomery reported that her guides told her a person in alpha receives images or symbols projected directly into their brain waves from the spirits and then that person reprojects those images and symbols as their own.

I remember once in a yuwipi ceremony of Dawson's that several Hebrew elders from Jerusalem were in attendance. One complained that he was clawed on top of his head by a spirit eagle and was bleeding. When the ceremony ended and the lights were turned on, he was surprised to find there was nothing wrong with him. Another time, a man named Rueben attended one of Dawson's yuwipi ceremonies and said that a buffalo spirit came to him, took his hand, and made him feel the buffalo head. Then the spirit blew snot into Rueben's hand. He told me he was going to save this mucous to show his wife as proof that he had been visited by the buffalo spirit. At the end of the ceremony when the lights were turned on, Rueben discovered that his hand was empty. I wondered if these two examples were what Montgomery referred to when she said that the spirits enter their throughts into your brain wave pattern, alpha, and then you receive these thoughts as your own. Can the spirits make you know and feel things that are actually not happening in the plane of what we call "reality"?

beta

alpha

theta

delta

Brain wave patterns are measured by a frequency measured in Hertz. 8-13 Hertz indicates a person would be in the Alpha state.

Up to this point in my research, I had felt that the spirit world and the collective unconscious were synonymous. After one of my workshops, a Paiute woman from Nevada went home and spoke to her grandfather about the material I had presented. He said that he, as a holy person, did not make contact with the collective unconscious; he communicated with the spirits themselves! This discrepancy bothered me for years. I was delighted to learn of Montgomery's information from her guides.

Right after that, I came across one of Cayce's psychic readings in which he was asked where he got his information while he was in a meditative state. Lythe Robinson, in *Edgar Cayce's Story of Origin and Destiny of Man,* said:

He gave two sources his mind apparently succeeded in tapping. One was the unconscious...mind of the subject himself; the other was what was called the universal memory of nature, Jung's Collective Unconscious, or the Akashic Records.

Cayce referred to the Akashic Records as the "Recording Angel." Was this contact with the Recording Angel actually contact with the spirits? Further investigations of psychic information revealed that the creative energy which exists throughout the universe is identical to the concept of the collective unconscious. Is this the reason for Dr. Jung's statement that the collective unconscious is common to everyone? If Jung's statement is true, then, indeed, we *are* all related. Is the revelation of these similarities coincidental or is it synchronistic?

Cayce, in answering a question about the difference between prayer and meditation, said, "Prayer is supplication to God, and meditation is listening to His answer." Meditation is used in nearly all the major religions of the world. I know that Native Americans receive messages from the spirits (God) in the following ways: the vision quest, the Sun Dance, the sweat lodge, religious races, yuwipi ceremonies, and sacred pipe ceremonies. Based on information researched thus far, I would feel comfortable in saying that these methods allow the holy man to enter into the alpha brain wave pattern.

Thomas Mails, in his book *Fools Crow*, stated that when Fools Crow performs the yuwipi ceremony, 405 helpers (spirits) come in, presenting themselves as sparks of light flying around the room. Cayce's statement that spirits are electrical in function seemed true, based on Fools Crow's experience in the yuwipi ceremonies.

Fools Crow continued his explanation: "The 405 powers are divided into four groups, each of which renders service in a given area." I was astonished at the similarities to the group mind concept about which Montgomery spoke. The four groups in Fools Crow's ceremonies, he indicated, provided services in the areas of plant medicines, helping people understand certain situations, dream interpretation, and helping to see within the bodies of men and other creatures.

In an account in *Lame Deer, Seeker of Visions* edited by Richard Erdoes, Lame Deer remarked, "While the *yuwipi* lies on the floor in his star blanket, his spirit could be hundreds of miles away in the far hills, conversing with the ancient ones." In the yuwipi ceremonies of Dawson No Horse, the main spirit was named Canupa Gluha Mani. Some people felt that this spirit was actually Dawson's spirit which had come out of his body.

Cayce said that if you can exhibit five qualities continuously for two cycles around the sun, then you have finished your evolutionary journey on earth, having become whole, and your spirit is free to leave your body at will. The five qualities are: brotherly love, peace, patience, long sufferance, balance/harmony. He also commented that if you can achieve one of these qualities for one cycle of the moon around the earth, then it becomes a part of you. When you have achieved all five for two years, you have attained a resonating oneness with that quality, and it is totally a part of you. Once you have achieved this oneness, when you talk, God talks; when you act, God acts.

Cayce said that Jesus was the first of mankind to complete his evolutionary journey on earth. He stated that Jesus was the man; Christ was the spirit within him. He made references to Jesus' healing powers, where he could heal without even touching the sick person. Cayce described it as the Christ spirit coming out of Jesus, doing the healing.

Upon reading this, I was reminded of a phrase in the Bible: "Know ye not that your body is the temple of the Holy Ghost which is in you, which ye have of God, and ye are not your own?"

In the teachings of Islam, it is said that Mohammed was not a savior, nor was he a messiah; he was simply a man through whom God spoke. If this is true, then had Mohammed become one with the total energy (God)?

In the Hindu belief, Krishna is presented with his female opposite, a symbol for wholeness. Had Krishna also attained oneness with the universe?

Cayce said that the book of Revelation was given to John in a vision. The person in the vision, according to Cayce, was John's own spirit (Holy Ghost), which had come out of his body and told him the information contained in Revelation.

The collective unconscious, speaking through Cayce, stated that the Christ spirit came to earth seven times: in Adam, Enoch, Melchizadek, Joseph, Joshua, Jeshua, and Jesus. I wondered how all these examples could be similar. Then I remembered something Jesus said: "Verily, verily, I say unto you, He that believeth in me, the works that I do shall he do also." I interpreted this--once again as in the "Original Teachings of the Red Man" chapter--to mean that all the things Jesus did are possible for us to do, too.

THE CENTER MOVED: A TRIAD OF CREATION STORIES

"The Center Moved" is a comparison of three creation stories: a Lakota creation story, a Hopi creation story, and a psychic interpretation of Genesis by Edgar Cayce. I was already aware of the Lakota and Hopi stories, but I did not know about Cayce's interpretation of Genesis until I "accidentally" stumbled across a book on it.

Each year after the Sun Dance, my family and I usually went to the Black Hills to rest for a couple of days before returning to where we lived in Denver. I remember after one particular Sun Dance, we were on our way to the Black Hills, when all of a sudden I got an urge to call my brother. I pulled over to a roadside telephone booth. My wife Dorothy asked, "What are you doing?"

I replied, "My brother Ken is trying to reach me."

"How do you know?" she asked.

"I don't know," I admitted. "It's just a feeling I have." I was unable to locate him after calling several places. Days later when we were back in Denver, my brother phoned me at home and asked, "Where were you on Monday?" That was the same day I'd had the urge to contact him!

As the years passed, I noticed that after each Sun Dance, there is a period of time when the Sun Dancer is on a "spiritual high," where such events as that described above seem to happen spontaneously. Sometimes the feeling lasts a couple of days, sometimes up to four days.

One year we had to return to Denver directly after the Sun Dance, forsaking our rest in the Black Hills. The very next day, I awoke early because I was so used to getting up early during the Sun Dance. I fumbled around the apartment, trying to occupy my time. Coming across a book called *Edgar Cayce's Story of Origin and Destiny of Man* by Lytle Robinson, I began reading about Cayce's psychic interpretation of Genesis. I could immediately see how it related to the Hopi and Lakota creation stories. Engrossed in the book, I was startled to hear a large boom and a rolling of thunder. I thought to myself, "I don't remember the weather forecast calling for rain." I got up and looked out the window. There wasn't a cloud in the sky! Returning to my reading, I noticed how the comparison of the three stories became more intricate. I will briefly tell each story and then identify the similarities among them.

In D/Lakota philosophy, it is believed that Wakan Tanka is at the center of the universe, symbolized by the sacred tree in the middle of the Sun Dance circle. The Sun Dance tree holds a nest at the point where the branches fork at the top. This nest, which is symbolized by cherry branches, represents the nest of the Wakinyan (thunder beings). In the creation story, as recorded by James Walker in *Lakota Belief and Ritual*, the creator is called Inyan. He was first, and at that time there was only darkness. He had a companion named Wakinyan. The story, related by Walker, says that Wakinyan co-existed with Inyan. But others say that Wakinyan was created by Inyan. (That Wakinyan comes from Inyan can be seen in the construction of the words: Inyan = Wak-Inyan.) The story continues that Inyan decided to create. First he brought into being Maka, the earth; then Mini, the water; then Mahpiyato, the powers of the universe--more commonly called the sky. In order to create these elements, Inyan used up all his power, then shriveled up and became hard. That's why Inyan is known today as the rock.

Maka, the earth, said, "I'm cold." She asked Inyan to warm her.

He said, "I can't. I used all my power."

She continued her complaints about being cold, so Mahpiyato said, "I'll warm you." He created Anpetu Wi, the sun; Tate, the wind; Hanhepi Wi, the moon; and the Pte People. (Pte is a Lakota word for female buffalo.) The Pte People lived underground. The Sun warmed Maka, the earth, and she felt better.

Now there was night, day, wind, water, but still no life. Wakinyan said, "Let me create the life." Wakinyan's voice is the thunder, the blink of his eye the flash of lightning. With a bolt of lightning, he created the fish, all the green things, the winged ones, and all the four-leggeds.

There was now life but still no man. There were only spirits on the earth at this time. One of the spirits was named Unk. She married her own offspring who was called Unkcegi. As a result of this incest, they created monsters called Unktehila that roamed the world.

The Pte People, ancestors of the D/Lakota people who dwelt underground, had a beautiful place to live, with no darkness, plenty to eat, no worries, and no troubles. A spiral cavern led up to the surface of the earth from this place. The chief of the Pte People was named Wazi and his wife was Wakanka. Their son was called Tokahe. One day Tokahe was wandering up the spiral cave. Nearing the entrance to the surface, he saw a wolf looking down. The wolf told him many tempting stories about life on the surface. Tokahe went and got his family, persuading them to come out of the spiral cave to live on the surface of the earth. Today they are known as the Lakota people.

The second story for comparison is the Hopi creation story, which comes from *Book of the Hopi* by Frank Waters. During initiation ceremonies, Hopi youngsters are told this story. In the center of the kiva floor is a hole, the sipapuni. (Original kivas were built in a circle which represented the universe. Today some kivas are built in square or rectangular shapes.) The sipapuni is identified as a place where the spirits emerge. The fireplace, representing the First World, is adjacent to the sipapuni on the floor. The pedestal where the ladder sits stands for the Second World. The ladder, used to enter the kiva, represents the Third World. When a person emerges from the kiva through the door in the ceiling, he emerges into the Fourth World.

The First World was Tokpela, endless space. At this time there was only the creator, Taiowa. "There was no beginning, no end, no time, no shape, no light. Just an immeasurable void that had its beginning, end, time, shape and light in the mind of Taiowa, the creator," narrated Waters. Then Taiowa created Sotuknang and told him, "You are to carry out my plan for life. You are my nephew and I am your uncle." Sotuknang then went out into the universe known as Tokpela, the First World. He created a helper and named her Kokyangwuti (Spider Woman), telling her that she was to remain on earth. Spider Woman, in turn, called into existence all the living things-- the green things, the water creatures, the winged ones, and the four- leggeds. Spider Woman looked at her creations and said, "I need to create a form in the image of Sotuknang." Thus, she gathered four colors of earth--yellow, red, white, and black, mixing them with the saliva from her mouth. Then she molded them, covered them with her white substance cape, and sang a creation song.

When she uncovered these forms, they were human beings. But they couldn't walk straight: they wobbled and staggered; they couldn't even talk, they just mumbled. She covered them again and sang the creation song. This time when she uncovered them, the Hopi humans stood before her. They had come from the underground.

The Hopi believe that they emerged from a place in the Grand Canyon and evolved through four worlds. To review, in the first world, man became wicked to the animals. Some people committed bestiality with the animals and created monsters. That world was destroyed by fire. Man became greedy in the second world, and it was destroyed by ice. In the third world, man misused technology, and a flood destroyed that world. Presently, we are living in the fourth world.

The third creation story is a psychic interpretation of Genesis. The Creator, as explained by Gladys Moore, is at the center of the universe, expanding outward into individual spirits. There are trillions and trillions of these spirits, yet there is only one, as recorded in Lytle Robinson's *Edgar Cayce's Story of Origin and Destiny of Man*. The Creator, then, made the universe in seven stages.

In Stage One, the spirit moved, the center moved. The story goes, "By moving itself out of itself [it] created a separate vibration [pattern]. Thus, into this sea of peaceful and harmonious vibrations, came Amilius." Amilius, the light, was the first expression of the Creator. Robert Krajenke, relating Cayce's interpretation in *A Million Years to the Promised Land* furthered Robinson's account, "For in the beginning, God said, 'Let there be light. Each of you are one of those sparks of light with all the ability of creation and all the knowledge of God.'"

In the second stage, Robinson continued, the Creator separated everything in the universe into matter and spirit. In Stage Three, the Creator gave all the spirits the power to reproduce. The fourth stage saw the Creator bringing all of the solar systems into being at the same time. The psychic readings say that the solar systems were created for man.

The Creator, in Stage Five, made all living things on the planet, the living beings in the water, the green things, the animals, and the creatures that fly. At this point, man was still non-existent. There was, however, a spirit named Lilith who was the forerunner of Eve. She occupied animal bodies and misused her sexual powers, producing a conglomeration of monstrosities. These monstrosities roamed the earth millions of years ago and have come down to modern man in the form of myths. A few names of these monsters are the centaur, the sphinx, and the satyr. Cayce commented that the passage in the Bible which refers to this time is, "That the sons of God saw the daughters of man that they were fair and they took them wives of all which they chose." Another passage referring to these times Cayce said was, "There were giants in the earth in those days." He further remarked that this is why the following passage appears in the Bible: "It repented the Lord that he had made man on earth and it grieved him in his heart."

Robinson, setting forth Cayce's material, stated: These monstrosities roamed the earth and they mixed with the animals. Sex was the determining factor as symbolized by the serpent. Through their offsprings, souls were being born again and again in a prison of matter from which they could not extricate themselves. Trapped in these grotesque bodies, man as such was drifting further and further away from his source. [the center]

In the sixth stage, the Creator decided to step in and straighten out this mess. He thus created Adam. "He created Adam as an individual as well as a group because Adam means man. Adam started the long journey back to the state of being worthy of and companionable to the Creator," stated Robinson's book. Man was given free will as a way for our souls to eventually become one with the Creator or to become whole, enabling us to complete our evolutionary journey on earth.

The readings reported that man was created in five places at the same time. To review, white men appeared in the Caucasus and in the Carpathian Mountains; the red man in North America and Atlantis; the yellow man in Mongolia; the black man in the Sudan and Upper West Africa; and the brown man in South America and Mu. The reason for five races, the readings further commented, is that the five senses of our material existence are represented. In the Bible it is told, "The Lord God formed man from the dust of ground and he breathed into his nostrils the breath of life and man became a living soul." Cayce's readings continued:

The time came when Adam as a race had to be divided into positive and negative or male and female. This division was necessary for the Adamic race to propagate perfect physical bodies through which the entrapped or lost souls could manifest and gradually find their way back to the source.

Information from the collective unconscious of Edgar Cayce revealed that the 5 races of man first appeared at these locations.

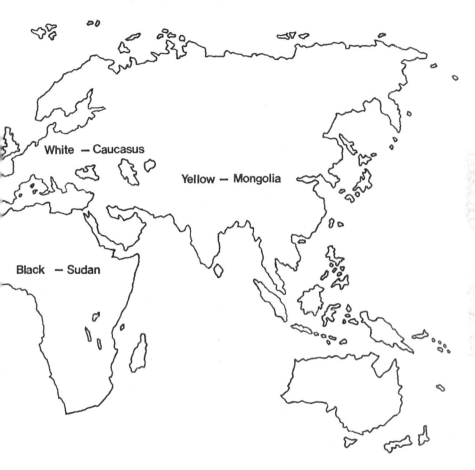

White — Caucasus

Yellow — Mongolia

Black — Sudan

(The reason the male is considered positive is that he is the penetrator and the female is the receiver. Thus, "positive" and "negative" should not be seen as good and bad.)

Adam, in the beginning, was both male and female. God made the separation into male and female from Adam so that reproduction could take place to provide the spirits with bodies they could occupy. "Eve was created to complete and complement Adam's male expression," the readings explained.

Robinson described the last stage: The seventh stage or seventh plane can be considered as one of contemplation and review. All that which was destined for the manifestation in earth plane had been perfected within itself in the mind of God. Now God's spirit flowed into these creations, giving them life.

Now let us begin the comparison of the three stories. In each story the creator started from the center of the universe. The first creations were: Wakinyan in the Lakota story, Sotuknang in the Hopi story, and Amilius the light in the Genesis story. Wakinyan, translated into English, means the source of thunder and lightning. In the Hopi story Sotuknang's symbol is lightning. Amilius, in the Genesis story, was the first spark of light.

I noticed that the Pte People, Kokyangwuti, and Lilith were all similar characters. Pte means female buffalo, Kokyangwuti was Spider Woman, and Lilith was the animal woman. Each story stated that sexual powers were misused, creating monsters. Another comparison among the stories is that creatures emerged out of the earth to become man.

The readings declared that Amilius the light, the first creation in the Genesis story, is known today as the Christ spirit. Reading this, I thought, "If Amilius the light is the Christ spirit, then so too are Wakinyan and Sotuknang." Do the D/Lakota and the Hopi have cultural linguistic names for the Christ spirit? I recalled that the nest of the Wakinyan is in the Sun Dance tree, and I wondered if there was a connection with the vision I had of Christ at the Sun

130

Dance. If, indeed, the Christ spirit has a cultural name, then this spirit must be in all cultures.

Another revelation came to me as I studied these stories. The readings of Cayce remarked that Amilius the light appeared as the five races of man, indicating that there were many spiritual patterns, yet there was only one. In D/Lakota theology, Wakinyan is also referred to as Wakinyan Oyate, the thunder beings, implying that there are many spiritual patterns, yet there is only one. I questioned, "Is the Christ spirit a group mind?" If this is true, then it makes sense to me that the Christ spirit could have appeared as Adam in five different locations. Is this why Jesus said, "Before Abraham was I am."? Pondering these similarities, I remembered the crash of thunder that came when I first began reading *Edgar Cayce's Story of Origin and Destiny of Man.* Had the Wakinyan

WAKINYAN
(powers that fly)

SOTUKNANG
(first power)

AMILIUS
(first spark of light)

These figures were identified as having cultural linguistic names for christ spirit

Oyate guided me to uncover these comparisons of the three creation stories? Was the discovery of the similarities coincidental? Or was it synchronistic?

Further contemplating these revelations, I recalled that when the D/Lakota use the sacred pipe, the first spirit they call into the ceremony is the Wakinyan Oyate. The Christ spirit is the first spirit that is called into the ceremonies. Is this the reason for so many miraculous healings in the ceremonies?

Another thought: in D/Lakota theology a man becomes a heyoka only after he has a dream or a vision of lightning. I remembered Dawson's first vision quest. On the fourth day lightning brought him his main spirit helper Canupa Gluha Mani. The Cayce readings said that Mary was chosen to give birth to Jesus during a ceremony in which a lightning bolt appeared directly in front of her. The psychic readings also revealed that a priest is chosen by the people, but a prophet is selected by God. Was Dawson chosen by God?

Information continued coming to me as a result of the comparisons. I mentally reviewed the sweat lodge ceremony and realized it was a genesis story. The sacred fire used to heat the rocks represents the eternal fire that burns at the center of the universe. The red-hot rocks are the Inyan, the Creator. They are passed into the sweat lodge in a sacred manner, then placed in the center. The sacred water is brought in and the flap closed. It is pitch-black in the sweat lodge, expressing the beginning of time. All that existed at that time were the spirits. The ceremony begins by calling in the Wakinyan Oyate.

The sweat lodge also acknowledges the pairs of opposites that exist in the universe. The elders say that if you want something good, you have to suffer for it. The individuals, thus, endure this steam heat while praying for good things for the people. When they finish their prayers and are about to emerge from the lodge, the leader reminds them that they are leaving the spirit world and are becoming like their brothers, the four-leggeds, crawling out

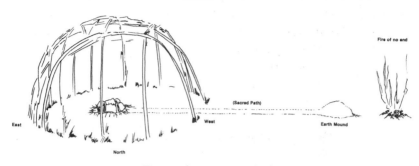

SWEAT

Fire of no end

(Sacred Path)

East

West

Earth Mound

North

Frame for a sweat lodge

the door to become two-legged man. In traditional D/Lakota theology, there is no holy book where people can read about a genesis, but they have a ceremony where they can actually experience the genesis story.

The Hopi ceremonies are continuous throughout the year. The first ceremony of the year is called Wuwuchim, when the young men and women are initiated into their clans. The initiates are taken into the kiva and the creation story is recited to them. They are allowed to re-enact the story, utilizing the objects within the kiva: the sipapuni, the fireplace, the pedestal, and the ladder. When the initiate is taken by his newly-adopted clan parents and rushed out of the kiva via the opening in the roof, an old man douses them with water, representing a cleansing as they enter the fourth world, the world of today. This ceremony allows the

133

Hopi initiates to experience the genesis story. Is this a right-brain approach to religion?

In the Hopi tradition, all newborn babies are given a rattle when they come into this world. Painted on the rattle is the swastika emergence symbol. The story is that when the Hopis originally emerged from the underground, Sotuknang was standing there handing out the clan duties and clan songs. He told the Hopi, "Don't you ever forget your clan duties or your songs to the Creator." In my way of thinking, this was the Christ spirit standing there telling them to always remember their clan duties and songs.

According to the previously mentioned readings of Cayce, the Christ spirit has come to earth seven times: as Adam, Enoch, Melchi zadek, Joseph, Joshua, Jeshua, and Jesus. I remember in my Bible school days, the teacher always mentioned that one day Jesus was going to return. Considering this possibility, I came across a book by Ruth Montgomery titled *Strangers Among Us: Enlightened Beings from a World to Come*, in which she asked her guides "...if Jesus of Nazareth would again reincarnate to prepare the body for the Christ spirit and the guide said He would not." I understand this to mean that the body of Jesus will not come back, but that the Christ spirit is returning. These words reminded me of a passage from the Bible referring to the returning of Christ: "Then two shall be in the field. One shall be taken and the other left. Two women shall be grinding at the mill. One shall be taken and the other left." Does this mean that only fifty percent of the people will recognize the Christ spirit when It returns?

A Mormon told me that in the next age, Christ and the Indians would lead the way. My mind formed questions: "Why were the Indians chosen to help lead the way? Is it because they still perform their ceremonies?" I know that many non-Indians are trying to find an answer by participating in Native American ceremonies,

134

but I remember what David Spangler wrote in his book *Conversations with John*:

You cannot become an Indian in the deep way that a person is born into that cultural pattern can. However, you can find correspondences within your own culture to the wisdom of the traditional peoples since your culture was once a traditional one as well.

In the Baha'i faith, Abdu'l-Baha, the son of Baha'u'llah challenged, in *Circle of Unity*, a proclamation to the Native Americans from the Baha'i faith, "You must give great importance to the Indians. There is no doubt that through the divine teachings they will become so enlightened that in turn to shed light to all regions of the world." Peter Nabokov, in an article entitled "America as Holy Land" printed in *Americans Before Columbus*, a publication of the National Indian Youth Council, reiterated Abdu'l-Baha's words:

I believe, as Carl Jung said, in one of the final letters of his life, when death approached and all the world's spiritual disciplines he had studied, he turned to the Native American and he said, 'We are sorely in need of truth and self-understanding similar to that of ancient Egypt,' he wrote. 'which I have found still living in Taos Pueblo.'

At this point in my life, the issue of the sacred Black Hills being the place of the origins of the D/Lakota people was becoming important. It wasn't until the summer of 1985 when I went for a vision quest on Bear Butte that I really got interested in the Black Hills being a location for the origins of the red man.

This was my second trip to Bear Butte. Frank Fools Crow presided, and Jim Dubray was a spiritual advisor. I had previously fasted under Dawson No Horse and Elmer Running at Pine Ridge and Rosebud. During this quest on Bear Butte, I had a vision which led me into further research on the three creation stories.

I had been on the hill for two days and two nights. It was the morning of the third day. The dawn had arrived but the sun had not yet appeared. I was preparing to leave the mountain. I knew that the helpers were coming to get me in a couple of hours. Until this time, I had had no dream or extraordinary experience. I had just finished praying with my pipe and looked to the south. Directly below me, the hills had turned red. I counted them; there were seven. I thought to myself, "The hills must be red because of the rising sun's reflection." I turned and looked to the east. To my surprise, the sun had not yet appeared. I quickly turned back, looked at the hills below me, and saw that they were still red. At that moment, a message came to my mind that said, "These red hills are the origins of the red man." I thought to myself, "This must be a vision, but I'm not going to tell anybody because no one will believe me." I felt people would say I was crazy.

The minute I promised myself I wasn't going to tell anybody, I gazed at the red hills and, right in the center, four deer stood up and began walking toward the east. When I saw them, I knew that their coming into sight had symbolic significance. (In D/Lakota theology the number four stands for the four sacred directions, and the deer represents the black tail deer spirits of the east.) In musing about the appearance of the deer, I was given another message: "You are supposed to tell your vision. That's why we gave it to you." I watched the deer disappear into the ravine and I knew I had to tell this vision, no matter what the people thought. I told it in the sweat lodge when I came down from my vision quest on Bear Butte.

There is a story that long ago the spirits came and told the D/Lakotas a flood was coming. Those who listened went up to Oblapaha (a high hill) to escape the water. Those who didn't listen stayed down below. The flood came and covered the people who remained below. When the water went down, their brothers came down from Oblapaha and began looking for them. They couldn't find their relatives and thought the flood debris had covered them up. They dug down into the earth, where they found a red rock. It is said that this red rock is the body and blood of our ancestors who died in the flood. The same red rock is the stone that we use to make our sacred pipes.

Another story we have linked with the red earth of the Black Hills is that long ago when one was initiated into the D/Lakota society, one's forehead was painted with this red earth we call wase, which was collected from sacred places. This painting of the forehead symbolized that the individual, who had been born in the beginning from the red earth, was being reborn into adulthood.

I also knew that the D/Lakota had origin stories connected with the Black Hills. Specifically, they say that the cave from where the D/Lakota emerged is Wind Cave in the southern part of the Black Hills.

In the psychic readings, Cayce talked about the red man appearing in North America and Atlantis. He said the color of the race was determined by the environmental and climactic conditions of these two continents. Ruth Montgomery stated in her book *The World Before* that the sole reason for creating five races was to help man cope with the climactic conditions. Man's appearance in North America and Atlantis was so that he could harmonize with the red clay of those continents.

After reading what Cayce and Montgomery said, I wanted to check other Native American origin stories. In *Seven Generations* by David Blanchard, the Mohawk Indian legend stated that when the earth was ready for the habitation of man, God went to the shore of a great lake and scooped up a handful of red earth and said, "Now I will make Onkwehanwe (human beings)."

Other stories I found came from *Spirits of the Sacred Mountains* by William E. Coffer. The Yakima origin legend asserted that God made man from a ball of mud, then told him what to do. The Natchez Indians specified that the Great Spirit molded the first man out of clay. The Pima said that God made the first man in his image from mud and placed him in the sun on the slopes of Baboquivre to dry. The story goes that the first time God took man down from the slopes, he wasn't done; he was too light. So God made another man and put him back out on the slopes. This time the man was left there too long, and he got too dark. The third time God made man and put him on the slopes, He waited until man was just right, a beautiful red color. The Spokane oral history related that in the beginning a great crash of thunder loosened a piece of red rock which turned into a handsome red man.

The Hopis, according to *Book of the Hopi*, believe that they emerged from the earth. The first being to emerge was called Kokoyemsin (mud head). His color was that of the red earth. The Hopis further believe they came out at the Grand Canyon. When I read this, I remembered Cayce saying, in the psychic readings, that when man first appeared in North America, the only area above water at that time was the mountain states. He addressed the Four Corners area specifically (the place where Arizona, New Mexico, Utah, and Colorado all touch) in one of his psychic readings as an area in which man originally appeared.

Because of my vision, my interest in an area for the origins of man centered around the mountains in western South Dakota. Geologists estimate that these mountains, known as the Black Hills, are among the oldest in North America. I speculated, then, on whether there was some physical evidence that might indicate a possible origin for man in the Black Hills.

One day while touring the mammoth site in Hot Springs, South Dakota, I came across the evidence I was looking for. Larry D. Agen broad, in a book on the mammoth site, diagrammed an area of exposed red earth which encircles the Black Hills. He called this area the Spearfish Formation and said it is part of the Triassic Period, estimated to be 230 million years old. Could it be that this red earth of the Black Hills was a site of origin for the red man?

My vision on Bear Butte told me that the red man appeared at that place. I reviewed a map that identified the location of the Spearfish Formation and found that Bear Butte was sitting right at the edge of this formation.

As I looked at this circle of red earth which surrounded the Black Hills, another Lakota creation story came to me. It's called the racetrack story. This racetrack encircles the Black Hills. A long time ago God created all the animals, the birds, and man to be equal. They lived in peace and harmony. One day they decided to have a race around the Black Hills to decide who would be chief of all beings. Man, the animals, and the birds all lined up at the starting line.

When they were given the signal to go, the deer took off and got way ahead of everyone. The buffalo followed close behind, and the turtle was a long ways back. The deer got so far ahead he sat down and waited. By this time, man was coming in about the middle of the pack and decided to make a deal with the magpie. He told the magpie, "If you win this race for me, I'll take good care of you."

The magpie said, "All right." He flew up and got on the back of the buffalo who was way out in front. Just as the buffalo approached the finish line, the magpie jumped up and flew across the finish line, winning the race for man. (That's why, in the Lakota way, man never eats a magpie.) Man was thus proclaimed chief of all the animals and birds. The race was so difficult that the runners' feet and hooves were rubbed raw, leaving a trail of blood around the Black Hills. That is why the racetrack is covered with red earth.

The earlier Lakota creation story tells that Wakinyan (lightning) created all life. I discovered an article about a biochemist named Dr. Stanley Miller and his colleague Harold Uray who had also used lightning, in a sense, to create life in a test tube. Their experiment included work with a "biological soup" made from substances they estimated existed in the early beginnings of the earth when there was no life. They applied heat to this soup until steam was created. Then they channeled the steam into a glass sphere, and when it was full, they sent an electrical charge into it. As a

139

result, they created the beginnings of life. They won a Nobel Prize for this experiment.

"Demonstrating that bits and pieces of life can be created by lightning and solar radiation from chemicals is one thing," said George Alexander in a November, 1982 *Reader's Digest* article entitled "How Life on Earth Began." He asked, "But how are these units assembled to manufacture proteins and genes?" He went on further:

Recent experiments have collaborated that mineral sheets of clay will concentrate organic molecules in a confined volume as water evaporates, orient them in ways that would facilitate linkups with other molecules and shield the fragile, newly formed compounds from destructive solar radiation. Israeli scientists have also used clays as catalysts to build short strings of amino acids--a first step toward fastening the very long chains of amino acids that we know as protein.

In related material, a section of the August, 1985 *Reader's Digest* called "News from the World of Science" reported:

NASA chemists have presented evidence that life on earth may have gotten its start in clay. They have shown that clays attract the organic molecules that make up protein and DNA, the in gredients of life, possibly from the sea during high tide. Clays might then trigger chemical reactions that string the building blocks into proteins and DNA.

I was excited to read that what these scientists theorized is exactly what the Native Americans and the Bible were saying in their creation stories!

Alexander continued in "How Life on Earth Began" by remarking, "Thus life, once begun, began to change, as in the symbiotic partnerships of different bacterial types to start what eventually became the animal, plant, and fungi kingdoms of today."

Each of the creation stories recounted earlier stated that man was created *after* the animals and the birds. Cayce's psychic readings divulged that man was created from animal. He specifically said that the spirits influenced the animal bodies by working through the endocrine glands to create man. This supposition put me in mind of the controversy today between evolutionists and creationists. Both try to prove their viewpoint is the one and only correct way. But according to the Cayce readings, in my way of thinking, both the evolutionists and the creationists' viewpoints are true.

In contemplating Cayce's description for the creation of man, I recalled my dream about the kiva representing the collective unconscious. In the Wuwuchim ceremony, the initiates emerged from the kiva to become Hopi. This movement from the collective unconscious to the conscious is also symbolized in the Lakota story of coming from the underground in Wind Cave to the surface of the earth to become the Lakota people. Is the Black Hills an origin site for the red man? Is it synchronistic that all these stories have come together at this time?

The way I see it, everyone has little pieces of information or pieces of the puzzle. The problem is that everyone wants their little piece to be the *only* piece. But if a person looks carefully, I believe it becomes obvious how all things are related.

THE POWER OF TELEKINESIS

Telekinesis is defined in the dictionary as "the movement of objects by scientifically unknown or inexplicable means, as by the exercise of mystical powers." I first came across the concept behind telekinesis when I was studying the history of the D/Lakota people, specifically in reading about the heyokas. The research stated that in the old days the heyokas had great power.

They were able to place their hands in a pot of boiling water containing a holy puppy and retrieve the head without being burned. The heyokas were also able to split the clouds in a rainstorm and cause the storm to go around. I learned, too, that in the old days, the only way one could join the Owl Feather Headdress Society was to be able to pick up a red-hot rock and carry it around the council tipi without being burned. And I heard that Crazy Horse wore a lucky stone around his neck to repel the bullets of the soldiers' weapons.

In the book *Sitting Bull, Champion of the Sioux: A Biography* by Stanley Vestal, a chapter entitled "The Bravest Deed of All" describes Sitting Bull and his people in a fight with some soldiers in the country of the Yellowstone River. The soldiers had taken shelter along the riverbank. Each time Sitting Bull and his men would attack, a number of them were wounded. He sensed that something was in the air; the situation just didn't feel right. Crazy Horse wanted to continue the attack, and many of Sitting Bull's young men wanted to follow Crazy Horse. Sitting Bull knew he had to do something in order to gain control of his men. He got off his horse, took his pipe, and went out in the middle of the battlefield between the Lakotas and the soldiers. Then he sat down and very calmly loaded his sacred pipe and started to pray. He did this for about fifteen minutes while the soldiers continued shooting at him. The bullets hit the ground all around him, but he himself could not be struck. After he finished praying, he slowly cleaned his pipe, returned it to his pipe bag, arose and walked back to his horse. When he returned to his warriors, they all shouted in his favor. Sitting Bull knew he had regained the confidence of his men. He told them, "We will fight no more today," and they left.

Learning of these achievements of the D/Lakota Indians, I discovered that other tribes also claimed individuals who could perform similar feats. A Cheyenne warrior named Roman Nose was given some "medicine" by the spirits in a ceremony. They told him that as long as he did not eat with metal utensils, he would be protected from the soldiers. Arden, a Zuni friend of mine, told me that in their sacred teachings, when a person has advanced to a stage where, during a ceremony, he is allowed to place an eagle feather in the sipapuni and the feather stands upright by itself, that person is considered a spiritual leader.

As described in "Original Teachings of the Red Man," it wasn't until 1974 that I actually experienced one of the phenomena mentioned above. At that time, I saw Frank Fools Crow split the clouds and make the rain go around.

Another time at a Fourth of July celebration at Wakpamani Lake, I witnessed a kettle dance in which Frank Fools Crow and Dawson No Horse placed their hands, without getting burned, into a pot of boiling water which contained a sacred puppy.

The Kettle Dance is a healing ceremony, in which the preparation is just as important as the ceremony itself. Once at Dawson's place I witnessed the preparation for this ceremony. A young puppy with no name and which didn't belong to anyone was selected. Steve Dubray rigged a rope to hold the puppy in the air between two men Sun Dancers. The rope was placed around the puppy's neck, then pulled tightly, lifting the animal into the air. A club which represented the Wakinyan, was lowered very quickly onto the puppy's head, killing it instantly. The rope around the creature's neck prevented it from crying out and also kept the spirit in the puppy. Since it was the Wakinyan symbology that killed the dog, it was felt that the Wakinyan spirit is the spirit that remained inside the animal. It was then prepared for the boiling kettle. When a holy man placed his hand in the kettle, it was to retrieve the puppy's head which was passed around to the sick people. Individuals, by eating the meat or even just touching the head, would be cured of their ailments.

Later that evening at the beginning of Dawson's yuwipi ceremony, he told people that the Kettle Dance was a very old ceremony. He said that times were changing and he thought many people didn't eat puppy meat any more. He remarked that even he didn't eat it.

An example of telekinesis was related at a conference I attended at the University of Nebraska where Thomas Mails (Frank Fools Crow's biographer) spoke. He had heard the story he told from a medical doctor who lived in Rapid City, South Dakota. A Lakota man was terminally ill. As a last resort, Fools Crow was called to the hospital to see what he could do. Entering the patient's room, Fools Crow sat in a chair and took off one of his mink braid wraps and began to pet it. At the same time, he started to sing a sacred song. All at once the mink came alive. It jumped down to the floor, ran across the room, jumped up on the patient's bed, and began sucking on the man's chest. A few minutes later, the animal jumped down from the man's bed and returned to Fool Crow's lap where he turned back into a braid wrap.

Evidently, the mink had sucked out the poison because the patient recovered.

Another time my family and I were at my brother Hepi's wedding. He was getting married in a traditional Lakota way, what we call getting married by the pipe. After the wedding feast, Dawson gathered the people together for a healing ceremony. He placed some herbs in a jar of water, praying over it. As he prayed, the water suddenly started to boil. In a matter of only a few seconds, it became a tea. Dawson invited any person with an ailment they wanted cured to step forward and drink some of the tea.

Another story related to me about Dawson by Robert Two Crow was that one time the helpers were preparing firewood to heat rocks for a sweat lodge ceremony. When they had completed stacking the firewood on the rocks and were going to light the wood with matches, Dawson said to leave it be. He prayed and then he said that the spirits would light the fire. People waited about twenty minutes, and nothing happened. Some of them started to return to their cars. Dawson remained at the fire pit. All of a sudden, smoke appeared and within a few seconds, the firewood burst into flame.

Sidney No Horse, Dawson's son, told me a story about one time when Dawson was on the hill fasting. On the last day, the people went to bring him down so he could conduct a yuwipi ceremony for them. He told them to return to the ceremony house and get everything ready. "The spirits will bring me down," he said. When the singers began their calling song, the spirits brought Dawson through the wall and laid him out on the altar. Dawson's son, Sidney, said he questioned how this had happened and wondered if his dad were some kind of magician who had performed a magic act.

When Sidney told me this story, I immediately thought of when Jesus walked through the closed door and the disciples couldn't believe it, asking, "Master, are you a spirit?" I am also reminded, once more, of Jesus' familiar saying, "Verily, verily I say unto you, He that believeth on me, the works that I do shall he do also."

I was watching the Johnny Carson Show on TV one evening. His special guest was Uri Geller, who had been a captain in the Israeli army when his powers of telekinesis became evident. He was studied by scientists and grew disillusioned by their skepticism about his powers. He went into seclusion for ten years. Once again, he felt the urgency to demonstrate his ability to people. Carson remarked that he understood Geller could bend spoons with his power and stop clocks, concluding with, "What are you going to do for us tonight?" Geller pulled out a compass, asking

Carson to examine it to make sure it was working properly. He placed it on the table and said, "I'm going to move the needle on this compass." The camera zoomed in on the compass. Geller started to concentrate and, in a very short time, the magnetic needle began to move.

In a remark made in *Strange Stories, Amazing Facts* put out by Reader's Digest, Geller said he "...could not explain his 'powers.' He said: 'I feel it must come from some external source...'"

Once when I gave a lecture on telekinesis, a boy came up to me afterwards and said, "This is the second time I've heard you speak on this subject. After the first time, I went home and placed a cup on top of the TV, sat down in front of it, and concentrated on it for almost an hour, repeating to myself, 'Move, cup! Move, cup! Move, cup!' and the cup never did move. What am I doing wrong?"

I told him that the D/Lakota philosophy is that the person doesn't move things; the spirits do the moving. He questioned, "What do you mean?"

I replied by telling him that I felt he was confusing telekinesis with psychokinesis, which is the mind moving things, rather than things being moved in a mystical way as described in the dictionary definition at the beginning of this chapter. I further remarked that in the Cayce readings, Cayce commented that within each of us is a part of the universal mind. When the individual achieves oneness with the universal mind, when God speaks, he speaks; when God acts, he acts. Likewise, in Native American ceremonies, the holy man acts as a channel for the spirits (universal mind).

The notion of a holy man being a channel came to me one time when I was in a ceremony of Dawson's. I had a bundle of items I had saved from the D/Lakota Nations Trades Fair when Fools Crow had split the clouds. In the ceremony Dawson asked, "What do you have in that bundle?" I told him I had cloth and plant items. Then I explained what Fools Crow had done, and he replied, "Fools

146

Crow didn't split those clouds. I did!" That statement baffled me for the longest time until I studied Cayce. Then I realized that it was not Dawson who was speaking. It was Wakan Tanka talking. During the time that I was still puzzled by Dawson's statement, I was working on "The Flowering Tree" for this book. One day the idea just came to me that the entire universe was a giant brain, and that half of it was left-brain energy and the other half was right-brain energy. I got up and told my wife, "Dorothy! Dorothy! Guess what just came to me? The whole universe is a giant brain." She covered her eyes with her hands and said, "Oh, no! No! Please don't tell anybody! If you do, they'll think you've flipped!"

Being a left-brain person, I needed to know if this was really true. I thought about returning to South Dakota and going to a ceremony to ask the spirits, but I was living in Denver at the time and the South Dakota trip was quite costly. I decided to ask a psychic instead.

I went to a person named Gladys Moore. I had prepared a list of ten questions. The brain question was the first one. The list was folded in my pocket. We sat down at the table where she had placed a block of wood that seemed to be in the shape of a Tao symbol (the curved line indicating the balanced parts of yin and yang) in the center of the table. She asked me to move my hands with hers in small circles on the surface of the table, remarking, "I don't really have to do this to make contact. I just do it for those who have a difficult time understanding or accepting what I'm doing. We don't have to do it if you don't want."

I said, "OK. I have a list of ten questions." I reached in my pocket and pulled them out.

"Don't show me the questions," she commanded. "Turn them upside down on the table. I will read each question and then answer it for you." To my amazement, she read and answered every one of my ten questions without even seeing the paper!

At this session, I learned from Gladys Moore that the entire universe was not a brain as such because a brain is a physical organ. Instead that the whole universe is made up of mind energy like that contained in the brain.

I became so enthused about Moore's information and the way she relayed it that I decided to go to one of her monthly meetings. It happened that the night I went to listen to her lecture, her topic was mind power. Once again I asked myself, "Is it coincidence or synchronicity that I am sitting in this lecture on a subject that I am studying?"

She said there are two directions in which mind power can be directed. First, the mind has a thought. Depending upon the thought, a certain response is dictated. If the thought is threatening, then you develop a fear. When you reach the point of fear, you may take one of two directions. One is where you start doubting. Then you start compromising. After that, you begin building a defense by making an excuse. That develops anger, and the anger destroys the mind power.

Here's an example: The thought you have is alcoholism. The response is, "Am I an alcoholic?" Fear develops about being an alcoholic. You begin coping with the fear by having doubts about whether or not you are an alcoholic. Then you compromise with yourself by saying, "Could I be an alcoholic? Maybe. Maybe not." You build a defense or make excuses, like, "I'm not an alcoholic. I'm a social drinker." Then you get angry over the whole alcoholism thought, which destroys the mind's ability to release the fear. You're now locked into a fear cycle.

Now, Moore said, when you reach the point of fear, ask your mind to release the fear. Just say to yourself, "Mind, release me from this fear of being an alcoholic." That develops a need to let go of the fear. Then you ask your mind to fill the need. You can say, "Mind, here's a need. I'll turn it over to you to deal with." Then you let it be. Instead of being locked into the fear cycle, you are able to release the fear of being an alcoholic. In Alcoholics Anonymous, it is said that if you have a problem, turn it over to your Higher Power and let the Higher Power deal with it.

I remember Dawson said, "Once you say your prayers, don't worry about them. If you worry about them, they'll just fade away." That brought to mind Jesus remarking that once we say our prayers, we should have faith in their being answered.

Mentally reviewing this example of how to use your mind power for telekinesis, I wondered how Dawson was able to perform his miracles. Did he make his requests to the spirits, then just let the matter be so the spirits did what needed to be done?

Pondering this question, I recalled an experience my brother Jim and I had at a sweat lodge ceremony. The two of us had just finished the ceremony and were drying off when I noticed that the water bucket contained deer horns. The deer horns were used to handle the hot rocks, and I had left them inside the lodge. I thought maybe Jim could have placed them in the bucket, and I asked him if he had. He replied that he hadn't. At that instant, we both felt that it was the spirits who had moved the horns.

Recollection of this incident made me consider, "If Dawson is one with the spirits, then he must be operating on the spirits' (God's) timetable." Was Dawson a spokesman for the spirits and a vehicle for their miracles at the same time?

The traditional way that Native American medicine people worked, when conducting ceremonies, was by request only, for positive purposes like healing or helping in some way. They didn't do these things to show off, and they did not charge a fee for people to participate. Traditionally, those who wanted to, gave donations to the medicine people. Everyone who had a need, however, could attend. If a person was sick, he could attend; if he needed help with a problem, he could attend. It was done this way because the medicine people realized it was not they who performed the miracles, but the spirits (God).

SACRED ABOVE IS LIKE SACRED BELOW

One summer I had returned to South Dakota from Denver to go on a vision quest with Dawson No Horse as my guide. I remember thinking as we were sitting watching the fire heat the rocks, waiting for a sweat lodge ceremony, "There is no pipe here. It seems like we should have a pipe with this ceremony. Maybe I should get mine." Just as I thought this, Dawson turned and looked at me. He stood up and came over to where I sat. He said, "Chuck, why don't you get your pipe and bring it so we can use it for our sweat lodge ceremony?" I didn't realize it at the time, but Dawson had read my mind. It was only after I returned home and reflected back on the experience that I comprehended what he had done.

Another time Rueben, an acquaintance of mine who lived in Denver, wanted to have Dawson conduct a ceremony for him. He gave Dawson some tobacco, but before he could make his request, Dawson said, "Ho, come in. Sit down. I know why you came." He began to tell Rueben why he was there. Not only did he explain that, he told Rueben he wanted to relate to him his own (Dawson's) life story. He started at the present day and worked backward. As Dawson began to tell his experiences, Rueben interrupted, "Hey, wait a minute! That's my life you're talking about."

Dawson said, "No, let me continue. I want to explain to you about my life." He went all the way back in his life's experiences to when he was two or three years old.

Rueben told me later what Dawson had done, "He said he was talking about his own life, but he wasn't. He was telling about *my* life. He mentioned things about my life that nobody knows. I haven't even told my wife some of what he told me that day." Rueben asked me how Dawson knew these things about him.

"Don't look at me," I said, "I don't know how he does that."

150

My brother Hepi told me about another experience he'd had with Dawson. They were preparing to go into the sweat lodge when Dawson went to the fire pit and picked up a red-hot rock. He turned and brought it to a twelve-year-old boy who stood there also preparing to go into the lodge. The boy took the rock, looked at it, then looked at Dawson. It didn't burn him. Dawson took the rock back and went into the sweat lodge and prayed with it. When he came out of the lodge, he told the boy the reason he could pick up that red-hot rock without being burned was that one day he would be "wicasa wakan" (holy man). But he said, "This ability will come to you only when you are older, not when you're fifty or sixty--but when you are an old man."

I began thinking about this incident. "There's a common denominator here," I reasoned. I pondered over the question for almost two years. Then I "accidentally" came upon the common denominator. Both Dawson and the boy were born in the same month. They were both born in March.

The revelation brought to recall the Cayce readings where Cayce talked about a study called astrology. The word astrology comes from the Latin and Greek and means star speech. According to Cayce, in between earthly lives, your spirit visits certain star systems, acquiring the vibration of that system. When it comes into the next body, it carries the vibration of that star system. The month you are born in identifies the star system your spirit had visited. Being a student of traditional Native American religious thought, I could accept what Cayce said about star systems having vibration. In the traditional D/Lakota philosophy, it is said that everything is alive. The earth is alive, the sun is alive, and the stars are alive.

As I studied this phenomenon, I remember reading about how modern scientists say that everything has a vibration. Everything contains atoms, and it is these atoms that provide the vibration of the object. Scientists say that rocks vibrate, for instance, but they're vibrating so slowly that they appear as solids. When you speed up the vibrations, the rock turns into a liquid. Speeding up the liquid vibrations eventually changes the liquid into a gas. The molecules are just vibrating at a different frequency. Traditional D/Lakota holy people say that the rocks are alive--that they contain a spirit. I wondered if the rock spirit and the rock molecules were the same.

Another example of the ability of rocks to contain vibration is found in the first radio. It wasn't run by electricity, nor was it run by a battery. It was operated by the vibrations put out by a rock. This radio was called the crystal radio. I became so intrigued with this idea that I even went out and bought a crystal radio kit. After a few minutes' effort, I had it operating. I was simply amazed at how a radio could be run by a rock!

Scientific discoveries that rocks contained vibrations just reinforced my belief that the stars are alive and the possibility of one's spirit acquiring vibrations from them even more believable.

It was at this point in my life that I wanted to acquire more knowledge on astrology. In visiting with my cousin Elgie Raymond and his wife Margaret, I learned that she was a novice astrologer. I asked her, "Where could I get hold of an astrologer who could teach me more about astrology?" She gave me the name of a New Age bookstore in Minneapolis. I called and asked if they knew of an astrologer who could teach me more about star systems, and they gave me the name of Joe Osowski. I phoned Mr. Osowski and found out that he conducted astrology classes. I made an appointment and flew to Minneapolis, proceeding to take some lessons from him.

Joe stated that there are many different kinds of astrology. I said, "Which one is the most common in the United States? That's the one I want to learn about." He introduced me to western astrology, which has a geocentric approach. After some explanations and discussions, I bought some books, went home, and started learning more about astrology. It took me a week to construct a birth chart, and at the end of that time, I wasn't sure that it was right. I called Joe, and he explained things to me over the phone. From that moment on, he became my continuing astrology teacher.

The first activity in constructing a chart is to identify which signs of the zodiac the planets are in and where they are from the horizon. The zodiac is a belt of star constellations that appears around the plane of the planets' orbits around the sun. There are twelve constellations that make up the zodiac. The stars of the constellations are positioned in such a way that they are seen to form symbolic objects. They are: Two Fish, a Ram, a Bull, the Twins, a Crab, a Lion, a Virgin, a set of Scales, a Scorpion, an Archer, a Goat, and a Water Carrier. Cayce said that each of these star systems has their own vibrations, each different from the other. Three of these symbols are associated with characteristics spoken of in terms of spiritual vibrations. The three are the Two Fish, commonly called Pisces; the Crab, known as Cancer; and the Scorpion, called Scorpio.

In astrology, it is calculated that if you were born from February 19th to March 22nd, you are known as having the sun in the sign Pisces, or as a Pisces. If your birthdate is between June 24th and July 24th, you are known as Sun in Cancer. If you are born from October 24th to November 22nd, you are called a Scorpio or Sun in Scorpio.

Cayce said in the psychic readings that if you were born during any one of those three times, one of the characteristics that will dominate in this life is spirituality. This gave me an idea. I decided to survey the Sun Dancers I knew to find out their birthdates. As I questioned them, I overheard one of them say behind my back, "What is Chuck Ross up to *now*?" The results of my survey showed that the majority of the Sun Dancers I talked to were born during one of the three times that Cayce outlined as containing spirituality. Since the D/Lakota religion does not proselytize for Sun Dancers, I wondered, "Was it being born with this spiritualism that led these dancers to participate?"

In reading *The Portable Jung* edited by Joseph Campbell, I found that even though Jung believed in synchronistic events, he had some reservations about astrology. He decided, therefore, to undertake a thorough investigation of astrology. As a result of his experiments, he was forced to recognize it. After reading this about Jung, I decided I, too, would continue my studies in astrology.

I found that once your spirit has been influenced by the stars and the closer it gets to earth's plane, it is next influenced by the planets. Just like the stars, the planets have vibration. Each planet vibrates at a distinct frequency. These frequencies then influence your spirit with dominant modes of thought. Nine planets and earth's moon are the major considerations in astrology. These are the planets listed in seriation from the sun outward: Mercury, Venus, Earth, Mars, Jupiter, Saturn, Uranus, Neptune, Pluto. These planets are not in a straight line. The first four are called the inner planets, and they move very fast in their orbits. It takes only a matter of months for them to revolve around the sun.

The remaining five planets, the outer planets, take years to revolve around the sun. When your spirit approaches Earth's plane at birth time, all of the planets are in different positions around the sun. Their position determines how the frequency influences your spirit. They appear in the different signs of the zodiac which have as their background the different constellations. The relationships between the planets are called aspects, which link planet energies together.

The stars, the planets, and Earth's moon are placed in certain positions on a birth chart, a map in the shape of a wheel with twelve spokes. The earth is at the hub, and the signs of the zodiac are on the circumference of the wheel at the points where the spokes touch the rim. Each zodiac sign occupies thirty degrees. While the constellations in the background vary in size, the overlap of the two changing over time is called the precession of the equinoxes. The sign Aries slowly precesses from Pisces to Aquarius as we progress to the age of Aquarius. The areas between the spokes are called houses.

If two planets are 60 degrees or 120 degrees apart, an easy aspect is formed. This means that the influence from these two planets would be easy for us in this life. Planets 60 degrees apart are called sextile, and those 120 degrees apart are known as a trine, and both sextile and trine indicate easy aspects. If there are three planets, each 120 degrees apart, this formation is called a Grand Trine. The influences from the combined three planets would be easy for a person in this life. If two planets are close together (within eight degrees), this is termed a conjunction, and the influence from these planets have a combined effect on your spirit. Two planets that are 45 degrees, 90 degrees, or 180 degrees apart are called difficult aspects. Influences between planets in these positions would have a more difficult effect on a person's life.

In order to plot a birth chart or star map, there are five things a person needs to know: the latitude and longitude of his birthplace, the day, month, year and time--down to the exact minute--of one's birthdate. With this information, one needs to consult an ephemeris, a book which contains tables giving computed positions of the stars, the planets, and Earth's moon. This information, when plotted, determines which constellations and planets are important in one's life. Some people say, "What star system were you born under?" or "What's your sign?"

Looking through the ephemeris, I wondered, "How long did it take man to develop this book of charts?" As I mused about how old astrology was, I recalled seeing in the movie "Marco Polo" that when Polo had gone to China in the 1270s, he discovered that the Chinese were using astrology--in fact, had been using it for thousands of years. When he returned to Europe and informed the people about what he saw and heard, they told him he was crazy.

As I continued my research in astrology, I learned that once I have plotted a chart and determined the planetary positions and aspects, then I needed to review a book of interpretations. What one first looks for when interpreting a chart is the ascending sign, which is the star system on the eastern horizon at the time of the birth one is looking at. Whatever was coming into ascendancy at the time of birth, according to the Cayce readings, was very important.

Reflecting back on the spirituality aspects within charts, I asked Joe Osowski if he would calculate by computer some charts on holy people who were born during the three times of the year that were interpreted by Cayce as possessing spiritualism. In addition to spiritual times of the year, Cayce also said that certain planets had specific spiritual qualities: the moon in a chart is interpreted as an individual having a natural ability to communicate with the unconscious mind; Uranus that the individual would have psychic powers; Neptune that the person is seen as being a mystic; and Pluto that the individual would possess a higher consciousness.

The first chart I asked Joe to do was Dawson No Horse. When I received it in the mail, the initial thing I noticed was that it contained a Grand Trine with the planets Pluto, Saturn, and Earth's moon. It also contained Mercury and Neptune in trine with one another. Additionally, Neptune was in conjunction with mid-heaven. The sign of Scorpio was on his Ascendant. Not only was the sun located in the constellation Pisces, but the earth and Sun were exactly lined up with the Super Galactic Center.

As I interpreted the planetary aspects on his star map, several things caught my attention. Mercury in trine with Neptune means he had the *ability to read the thoughts of others*. I knew for a fact he could do this. The moon in trine with Saturn signifies that he possessed *organizational ability*. This reflects Dawson's ability as an Episcopal priest and a Lakota leader of sacred ceremonies. The moon in trine with Pluto indicates that he had the *ability of telekinesis*. Neptune in conjunction with mid-heaven means that

156

his profession would be *an occult profession*. The sign of Scorpio on the ascendant shows that the individual will *work to improve the status quo and for regeneration*. In Dawson's chart the earth in relation to the sun was lined up exactly with the longitude of the Super Galactic Center in the first degree of the sign Libra. That his chart inter pretations described him so well forced me to ask the question, "Was it coincidence--or synchronicity?"

I continued my research on holy men. Another chart obtained for me by Joe was on King David Ben Jesse, born on October 28, 1062 B.C. in Bethlehem, according to the research of Don Jacobs. As I reviewed his chart, the obvious thing that grabbed my attention was the two Grand Trines equally spaced on the chart. One contained the moon, Mercury, and Jupiter; the other Venus, Mars, and Pluto; with Pluto in conjunction with Saturn as well. The sun was located in the constella tion Scorpio. The stars of Leo were on his ascendant.

Going over the interpretations for these aspects, I found that Mars in trine with Venus means that he would have *a talent for music*. I remembered from my Bible school teachings that David played the harp and was an excellent singer. Mars in trine with Pluto indicates that the individual *would have no pity when fighting and could use spirit forces for the benefit of humanity*. Once again, I remembered that David killed Goliath with one stone. Mars in trine with Saturn denotes *military leadership, great stamina and strength under stress*. David, in his later years, I recalled, was a general. Saturn in trine with Venus means the person would *possess a sense of justice and would be willing to help others*. The stars of Leo on the ascendant shows that the individual is *ruled by his heart and exhibits authority*.

I have addressed here only the highlights in the two charts. There are many more influences that an experienced astrologer could identify by looking at these same charts. Being a novice, and yet being able to recognize that the charts had identified these individuals, had a profound effect on me.

157

STAR MAP

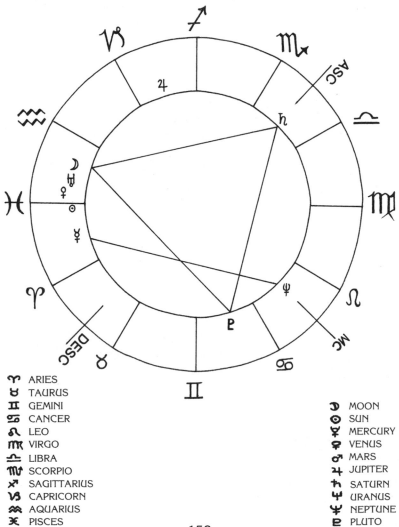

♈ ARIES		
♉ TAURUS		
♊ GEMINI		☽ MOON
♋ CANCER		☉ SUN
♌ LEO		☿ MERCURY
♍ VIRGO		♀ VENUS
♎ LIBRA		♂ MARS
♏ SCORPIO		♃ JUPITER
♐ SAGITTARIUS		♄ SATURN
♑ CAPRICORN		♅ URANUS
♒ AQUARIUS		♆ NEPTUNE
♓ PISCES		♇ PLUTO

158

STAR MAP

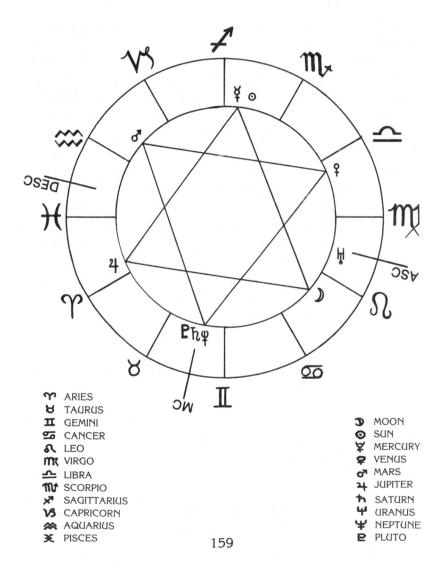

Another chart I received from Joe was on Frank Fools Crow. In the book *Fools Crow* by Mails, his birthdate was given as June 24th, but Fools Crow could not remember the year he was born, though he knew it was between 1890 and 1892. In discussion with Joe over the tele phone, he told me we could try to do a rectification in order to approach a workable birth chart.

The rectification process used in this case was to do a chart for June 24th for each of the three years. When I saw the three charts, I found that it would have been impossible for a man with Fools Crow's spiritual abilities to have been born in 1890. In reviewing the two remaining charts--which contained a nearly equal number of easy spiritual aspects--the chart for 1891 seemed to be the most accurate because of the position of the moon. This chart showed the sun in the constellation Cancer and Cancer also on the ascendant. The sun was also trine with Uranus. Mars was in trine with Jupiter, and the moon was in trine with Venus, Pluto, and Neptune. Jupiter appeared in conjunction with mid-heaven. Mars in trine with Jupiter means that the individual will *help the poor and help humanity*. The moon in trine with Neptune demonstrates having *strong psychic abilities*. The moon in trine with Pluto means the person will possess *powers of telekinesis*. The moon in trine with Venus indicates *sympathy for others* as a characteristic. The sun in trine with Uranus means that the individual can *tap the universal mind*. Jupiter in conjunction with mid-heaven shows the person as *a religious leader*. Choosing stars of Cancer for the ascendant interprets as possessing qualities of *sensitivity and diplomacy*. Again, I have interpreted only some of the factors in what appears to be Fools Crow's chart.

Another important chart that I requested was the Don Jacobs chart for Jesus. Joe had obtained this chart and the King David chart from information he had gotten from an article by Don Jacobs entitled "Astrology's Pew in Church" in the journal *Astrology Now*. In order to determine a birth time for Jesus, some rectification methods were again used. The chart had to have in it the

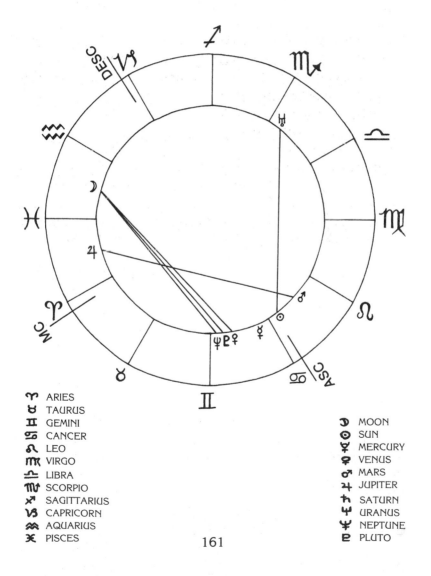

STAR MAP

FOOLS CROW
JUNE 24, 1891
Porcupine, S.D.

♈ ARIES
♉ TAURUS
♊ GEMINI
♋ CANCER
♌ LEO
♍ VIRGO
♎ LIBRA
♏ SCORPIO
♐ SAGITTARIUS
♑ CAPRICORN
♒ AQUARIUS
♓ PISCES

☽ MOON
☉ SUN
☿ MERCURY
♀ VENUS
♂ MARS
♃ JUPITER
♄ SATURN
♅ URANUS
♆ NEPTUNE
♇ PLUTO

161

7 B.C. Jupiter-Saturn conjunction, with the Sun, which is thought to have been what the Magi (wise men) followed. The birth time, arrived at in this way, fit marvelously for March 1, 7 B.C., Julian Calendar. The psychic readings of Edgar Cayce also stated that Jesus was born in March. The Church of Jesus Christ of Latter Day Saints believes that Jesus was born in the spring. Sid Hurlburt commented, in a *USA Today* article, that the early Christians did not really know when Jesus was born but decided to mark the date as December 25th to coincide with the winter solstice, in the hope of converting the traditional peoples who held their ceremonies at this time of the year.

As I looked at the chart, the first item that caught my eye was that there were four planets and the sun in conjunction with one another, lined up with the earth, Pluto, and the Super Galactic Center. The sun and planets group were in alignment with the sign Pisces and with the stars of Pisces, which in those days were in the same direction. The five bodies in conjunction with one another were the sun, the moon, Jupiter, Saturn, and Uranus. These five were also in trine with Neptune. Neptune was in sextile to Pluto, and Pluto was opposite the five bodies in Pisces, as well as in conjunction with mid-heaven which is aligned with the Super Galactic Center. (Don Jacobs did not mention this extremely important conjunction with the Super Galactic Center longitude.) The stars of Sagittarius were on the Ascendant. Uranus in trine with Neptune means the individual would have *ESP or clairvoyance*. Jupiter in trine with Neptune indicates *generosity and a wandering life*. The moon in trine with Neptune demon strates *strong psychic abilities and insight about the future*. The sun in trine with Neptune shows the person possessing *universal love, being a spiritual guide, and having the ability to heal others*. Saturn in trine with Neptune signifies that the individual will be good at *meditation and clairvoyance*. Neptune in sextile to Pluto means *mysticism and interest in reincarnation*. Pluto in conjunction with mid-heaven indicates *occult profession and spiritual mission* as characteristics.

The sun in conjunction with Jupiter denotes the individual will have a *positive outlook and be generous.* The sun in conjunction with Saturn marks the person with *good organizational abilities.* The sun in conjunction with Uranus designates that the individual will be a *genius and will understand universal law.* The sun in conjunction with the moon points out that the person will be *active with children.*

The moon in conjunction with Jupiter shows *sympathy and generosity and that the individual will be a messiah.* The moon in conjunction with Saturn means *common sense and hard working capability.* The moon in conjunction with Uranus demonstrates *intuitive abilities and an unusual family life.* Jupiter in conjunction with Saturn means the individual will be *at the mercy of a large social issue.* Jupiter in conjunction with Uranus indicates the person's interest *astrology and in being a reformer.* Saturn in conjunction with Uranus points to *an interest in the occult and that there will be danger to this individual's security.* Pluto, Earth, Sun, Uranus, Saturn, Jupiter, and Moon all lined up with the Super Galactic Center shows *extremely strong connection with the highest cosmic organizing principles.*

In studying the chart, I saw that Pluto was opposite the five bodies: the sun, the moon, Jupiter, Saturn, and Uranus. The sun opposite Pluto is seen as the individual *attempting to transform the world to their view.* The moon opposite Pluto denotes that the person will have a *tendency to influence friends toward new thought.* Jupiter opposite Pluto designates a *tendency to indoctrinate others to the individual's views.* Saturn opposite Pluto means the individual will have a *fated death.* Uranus opposite Pluto signifies *fanaticism in occult interests.* The stars of Sagittarius on the ascendant show that the individual is *concerned with the well-being of society and places spiritual law above self.*

163

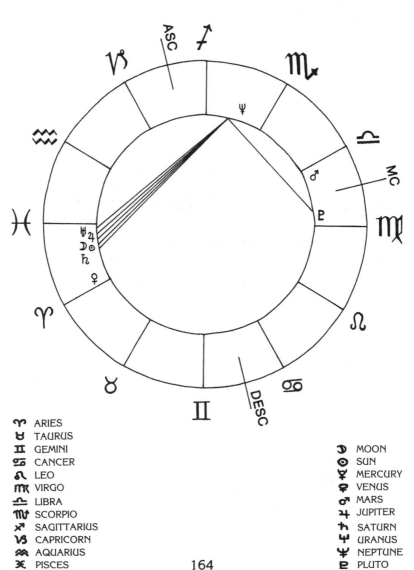

STAR MAP

♈ ARIES
♉ TAURUS
♊ GEMINI
♋ CANCER
♌ LEO
♍ VIRGO
♎ LIBRA
♏ SCORPIO
♐ SAGITTARIUS
♑ CAPRICORN
♒ AQUARIUS
♓ PISCES

☽ MOON
☉ SUN
☿ MERCURY
♀ VENUS
♂ MARS
♃ JUPITER
♄ SATURN
♅ URANUS
♆ NEPTUNE
♇ PLUTO

Joe pointed out to me that both Dawson and Jesus had the sun and earth at their birth closely lined up with the Super Galactic Center. The Super Galactic Center, he said, is that direction, now at tropical longitude of degree 39 minutes Libra, which is considered to be the center of the known universe. If the hypothesis that creative energy originates at the center is true, then I reasoned that the center of the universe would contain a higher order of spirit energy. I further contemplated that such spirit energy would have a major influence in Dawson's and Jesus' earthly lives. Is this the spirit energy that telekinetically transported Dawson's body through the wall? Is it the same energy that conveyed Jesus' body through a closed door?

Poring over literature on Jesus and astrology, I came across an article in the journal *Welcome to Planet Earth* entitled "Astrology and the Bible" by Steven Forrest. Forrest stated that the three wise men came from the east to Jerusalem and asked King Herod for the newborn who was to be king of the Jews. They said they had seen his star in the east and had come to worship him. Forrest found a problem with this, for he said that the wise men had come from the east. But to travel to Bethlehem, they would have to go west. "Yet," he quoted, "they saw Christ's star in the east, and followed it." He asked, "How could they go east and still arrive in westerly Bethlehem?" He continued by saying that there is no problem with this if one accepts that the wise men were astrologers. In astrology, both at that time and now, east is considered the ascendant on a chart. He said:

The wise men had seen Christ's 'star' on the ascendant in a chart they had erected. That's what the word means, not that there's an error in the text or that wise men were history's poorest navigators!

I went on with my research and found another article on this subject in the Reader's Digest *Strange Stories, Amazing Facts*. In an article entitled "Three Wise Men and a Star", it is said that:

The late Jesuit scholar Cardinal Danielou...considered the Magi's statement, 'We have seen His star in the East,' to be an allusion to a star at its rising, or in the ascendant--the most important factor in casting any horoscope. [birth chart]

Danielou continued by affirming that astrology was widespread among the Jews at the time of Jesus' birth, and "This is perhaps what the Magi, or astrologers, were doing when they visited Herod."

I remembered that once, immediately after I had finished a presentation on astrology, a young lady approached me and said she'd just returned from Israel. She had visited an ancient temple at Beth- Alpha which had only recently been excavated. She said it was located on a kibbutz in the northeastern part of the country. On the floor of this ancient synagogue was an astrological wheel or chart. She remarked that the tour guide's explanation had to do with something totally disassociated from astrology; but she herself knew that the wheel was an ancient astrological chart.

In studying astrology, I found that a person's chart indicates his inclinations at birth. From that moment on, one's free will, culture, and environment can influence this birth energy--making it possible to transcend one's birth chart. Cayce said, in a psychic reading, as quoted by Margaret H. Gammon in *Astrology and the Edgar Cayce Readings*, "Let it be understood here that no action of any planet or phases of the sun, the moon, or any of the heavenly bodies surpass the rule of man's will power."

If a person has a tendency in his chart to recognize negative qualities in situations, he has the free will to develop his ability to recognize the positive qualities in situations as well. (Cayce, incidentally, was born on March 18, 1877, one of the times of the year when a person possesses spiritual qualities. It is also interesting to note that both Dawson and Jesus were born during these high- spiritual-quality times of the year.)

I found, in continuing to delve into astrology, that a person's birth chart is much like a mirror. It identifies both his easy aspects and his difficult ones. An astrologer can ascertain the identification of many aspects about which an individual is not consciously aware. Once the difficult aspects have been identified, then the person has the free will to change them. The ultimate outcome is that he can transcend his chart. It's another way of becoming whole.

For me personally, not only have I been working on correcting the negative qualities in my chart, but I also realized that every chart is different. Such a consideration has helped me to develop respect for every individual. For example, my twin daughters Dana and Dawn were born one minute apart. We did a chart on each of them and found that they were different from each other, even though their birth times were so close together.

Another use I found for astrology was that of identifying career aptitudes for individuals. When my youngest daughter Sandy was a senior in high school, I asked her, "What are your plans for the future?"

She replied, "I don't know." I gave her a couple of weeks to think about it and repeated my question. She still responded that she didn't know. I decided to do a chart on her. When I looked at it, I found some interesting characteristics that I liked as a career objective for her. I phoned her to talk about this and was surprised to hear that she wanted to study architectural drafting. I felt let down because I wished her to study chiropractic, which I felt was a dominant theme in her chart. Having developed respect for each individual's chart, though, I quickly reviewed hers again and found that it said she would do well in any of the artistic endeavors. Her career choice was in her chart, and it was something she wanted to do. I decided to respect her decision.

In researching additional uses of astrology, I came across a paper put out by Sinte Gleska College entitled "Lakota Star Knowledge and the Black Hills" by Ronald Goodman. He said:

Mr. Stanley Looking Horse, current holder of the original Sacred Pipe at Green Grass on the Cheyenne River Sioux Reservation, has said, 'When our grandfathers came onto the reservation they had three things: two hides and sticks. One hide was a star map. The other hide was an earth map marked with hills, rivers and buttes. These two maps were the same because what's on the earth is in the stars, and what's in the stars is on the earth. The sticks were for time, measuring time...' Thus, Sacred Above is like Sacred Below.

The paper went on to disclose that the traditional Lakotas used the appearance of certain star systems to coincide with the location and time of their ceremonies. For example, Goodman said that when the sun is in the constellation Pleiades, the people will be in the Black Hills at Harney Peak to perform a ceremony welcoming back the Wakinyan Oyate. According to this paper, the Pleiades is the head of a buffalo which appears as an outline in the stars, with the three stars of Orion as the backbone, Betelgeuse and Rigel the ribs, and Sirius the tip of the tail. Goodman felt that the only time the Lakota people could have developed their ceremonies with the synchronized movements of the stars was 3,000 years ago. This is based on the procession of the Equinox, where each constellation is calculated to advance thirty degrees approximately every 2300 years. In the book *Mexico Mystique: The Coming Sixth World of Consciousness* by Frank Waters, he stated that in the astrological age (2000-4000 B.C.): All the great nations of antiquity arose--Egypt, Sumeria, Babylonia, and Assyria. Taurus the Bull was the earthly sign and the cult to the bull prevailed, as attested to the great bull monuments erected in the palace of Sargon II of Assyria, the Egyptian Apis of Memphis, and the Minotaur of Crete.

When I read this, I wondered two things: "Is this the same period when the buffalo star figure came into prominence among the Lakota?" and, "Was the end of this Taurus cycle concluded by Moses receiving the Ten Commandments and returning to his people and telling them no longer should they worship the golden cow?"

168

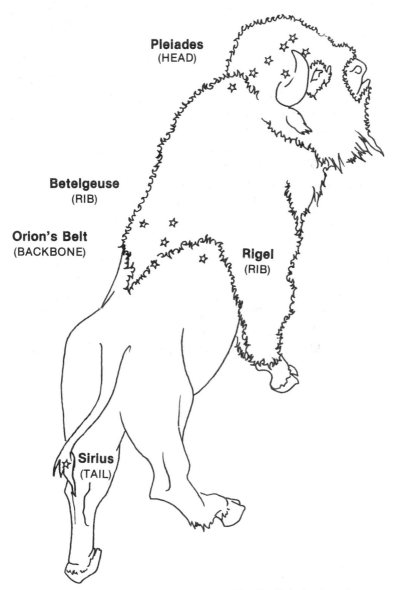

Pleiades
(HEAD)

Betelgeuse
(RIB)

Orion's Belt
(BACKBONE)

Rigel
(RIB)

Sirius
(TAIL)

These stars which portray a sacred White Buffalo in the sky were used to determine the time and place of lakota ceremonies.

Another work by Waters, *The Book of the Hopi*, stated that the Hopi also used the position of star constellations to determine the time for their ceremonies. I was pleased to know that traditionally Native Americans used the energy of the stars to aid in the performance of their ceremonies. This study of modern astrology has helped me discover an answer to the American Indian stories on star origins.

Once when I was lecturing to an anthropology group at the University of Minnesota on the five origin stories (American Indians came from the underground, from the stars, from an island in the west, from an island in the east, and originated in North America), a member of the group said, "Which story is true?" I told him all five were true. The stories only needed to be placed in chronological order. First, we came from the stars, as supported by astrology. (These are allegorical stories representing our spirit origins.) Second, we came from the underground (an allegory which relates how man moved from the collective unconscious upward into consciousness). Third, we have always been in North America, as supported by the psychic Edgar Cayce and others in this book. Fourth, we came from an island in the west, as validated by Cayce and others in this book. And fifth, we came from an island in the east, as indicated by Cayce and others in this book.

In my search for the origins of my tribe, I inadvertently discovered the origins of man. I have become cognizant that many different disciplines of study are interwoven. Indeed, "we are *all* related."

THE PURIFICATION

Searching the oral history for the origins of the red man, I came across many other legends. In the D/Lakota belief, there is a story that each leg of the white buffalo represents an age which mankind has evolved through. The four ages, according to the *Sinte Gleska College News* series (Rosebud, South Dakota) on the D/Lakota oral history, were the Rock, the Fire, the Pipe, and the Bow.

The Hindus in India have an almost identical legend. They say that each leg of their sacred white bull, Nandi, represents an age. Each age is called a yuga. Both the D/Lakota and the Hindu stories declare that we have come through three ages, and we are now in the fourth age, very close to the beginning of the next one.

The Navajo oral history also confirms that mankind must evolve through four worlds or ages. The first world was colored black and its symbol was mist; the second, blue with the bluebird for its symbol; the third, yellow and the symbols were man, bluebird, coyote, and bug. The fourth world is called glittering and the symbol is the locust. The Navajos, too, believe that man evolved through three ages and is now in the fourth world, the age of the glittering world.

The Hopi, as well, believe that man has evolved through four worlds. In the first world, man became wicked toward the animals. Because some of mankind were committing bestiality with the animals, the creator destroyed that age with fire. The Hopi who had maintained their sacred ceremonies went underground to survive the fire. In the second world, man became greedy, and the creator destroyed this world with ice. Those Hopis who had maintained their sacred ceremonies went underground to escape the ice. In the third age, man developed a high level of commerce, trade, and technology. He also had the ability to fly. His misusing this technology created a war that caused a great flood which destroyed the world. Those Hopis who had maintained their sacred ceremonies once again were able to go underground to

171

cape the flood. Then they emerged in the fourth world, the age of today. The Hopi believe, as do other tribal groups, that we are approaching the beginning of a new world.

When I read about how the Hopi believed we had the power to fly in a previous world, that brought to my mind D/Lakota oral stories which state that long ago the Santee had the power to fly. I wondered if this story was a reference to the third age the Hopis talked about.

Another reference to early peoples being able to fly came in a picture I saw when I was studying the Mayan culture. The photograph is of a coffin lid inside a pyramid at Palenque. It depicts a man at the controls of a flying machine. I also came across a Mayan legend which said that at one time the Mayans had the ability to fly. I wondered, once again, "Is this evidence for the existence of the third world?"

On the plains of Nazca in Peru, archaeologists have discovered giant etchings on the desert floor, several of which appear to be ancient landing strips. Erich Von Daniken, in his book *Chariots of the Gods*, declared that these landing strips are evidence of UFOs landing on Planet Earth. My reply is, "There are reports of UFOs landing today and they don't need landing strips." I mused about whether such ancient landing strips were part of the third world in which the Hopis say we had flying machines. I don't know.

In Bogota, Colombia, anthropologists have found ancient insect like artifacts. They labeled them as "bugs," and it wasn't until recently that modern man began to take a second look at them. Now they think that these artifacts are really model aircraft. Some of these insect like artifacts were taken to an aircraft designer to get his opinion, and he felt that many of them had, indeed, the design of an aircraft. They are estimated to be over 3,000 years old.

An artifact with the appearance of a bird was located in Egypt. Such artifacts have been called bird symbols over the years, but now anthropologists are re-examining the data. They think the symbols are ancient aircraft. My question is, "Are these ancient aircraft designs remnants from the third age when mankind had the ability to fly?"

In Bagdad, Iraq, archaeologists have found an ancient electrical battery which they estimate to be nearly 5,000 years old. When I went to school, I learned that mankind didn't develop the electrical battery until this century. Now it is shown that mankind had electricity nearly 5,000 years ago! Where did these ancient batteries come from? Are they more evidence for the existence of the third age?

Ancient spark plugs in California were uncovered. Their estimated age is 50,000 years old. I questioned, "What need would a primitive Indian have for spark plugs?" As soon as I asked myself this question, the legends of previous ages entered my mind. I felt pride that American Indian legends contained an answer to many of the mysteries of the modern world.

A surgeon and professor at the University of Ica, Peru, Dr. Javier Cabrera Darquea discovered ancient petroglyphs which he gauged to be nearly 50,000 years old. One of the etchings in the book *The Mysteries of the Andes* by Robert Charroux portrayed an American Indian with a feathered headdress scanning the heavens with a telescope. I was taught in school that man didn't study the heavens until Galileo used a telescope for that purpose. These petroglyphs implied that somebody was doing it 50,000 years ago!

Another petroglyph had an etching of three individuals with feathered headdresses performing a heart transplant. Modern man didn't complete a successful heart transplant until about 1975! What do these rocks depict? Are they stories that portray a previous age? Why do the etchings reveal the same story as our oral history about the third age? Is it coincidence? Or is it synchronicity?

Yet another petroglyph discovered by Dr. Cabrera portrayed ancient Indians performing a brain transplant. My first thought was that modern man hasn't even attempted a brain transplant yet. But the petroglyphs indicate that someone was doing it over 50,000 years ago. How else would the ancients have gotten the idea to carve it on a rock unless it had actually happened?

The ancient Mayan society had an ideogrammatic language. They used petroglyphs to transmit their messages. They also developed a high level of mathematics. They developed the zero a thousand years before the Arabs, and the Arabs had the zero a thousand years before the Europeans. In the Mayan system of numbering, a dot was 1, a dash was 5. The zero was described graphically as an oblong circle. If one found markings of a dot above a dash, that indicated the number 6; markings with three dashes meant 15.

The Mayan Indians devised the most accurate calendar in the history of the world. Their ancient calendar is almost five times more accurate than the Gregorian calendar we use today. How were these ancient people able to develop such a precise calendar? The thought entered my mind again, "Maybe the ancient Mayan calendar was developed during the third age." Then did we destroy ourselves and have to start all over?

When the Europeans first arrived in the Americas, did they not understand the American Indian because the Native Americans were apparently far superior in psychic abilities?

The Mayan calendar was based on the rotation of two wheels, one containing thirteen numbers, the other twenty numbers. The two wheels were meshed together in the fashion of cogwheels in machinery. The wheel with thirteen cogs stood for thirteen levels of heaven, and the wheel with twenty cogs represented twenty days to a month. If you were to spin these wheels around, they'd have to go around 260 times before they would match up again. This 260 cycle is called the sacred calendar to the Mayans. It was this calendar that was the basis for all other Mesoamerican calendars.

174

One of these Mesoamerican calendars, in particular that of the Aztecs, was discovered in Mexico City when the earth was excavated to build a new skyscraper. It is circular in design, weighs 25 tons, and is twelve feet in diameter. A historian by the name of Tony Shearer deciphered the inscriptions on this calendar and found that it, too, had a 260-day cycle. He also decoded the intricate workings of the calendar which revealed a 52-year cycle. By using the 52-year cycle, he was able to determine that this stone calendar portrayed five long cycles or ages for the ancient Aztecs. He also concluded that a new cycle would start on the Gregorian calendar date of August 16, 1987. He said that the information from the calendar disclosed that we were ending a negative cycle and we would be moving into a positive cycle. An etching of two figurines wearing headpieces, each headpiece resembling a single horn, was at the bottom of the calendar. Above the headpieces were symbols for the seven stars of the Pleiades. The Aztecs called these two figurines the Creator Twins, whom they believed came from the Pleiades.

When I heard this story, I recalled the Two Horn Society of the Hopis. The Hopi priests wore headpieces very similar to those worn by the Creator Twins of the Aztec calendar. Members of the Two Horn Society are the keepers of the creation stories which are told when the seven stars of the Pleiades are directly overhead at midnight. At that time, too, the Two Horn Society sings a set of seven creation songs. The Hopi also believe in spiritual origins from the stars.

The Hopis say that soon mankind will be entering a new age. It will be identified when the twins who hold the planet in balance can no longer accomplish their task. They call this the purification.

Almost a hundred years ago a Paiute medicine man named Wovoka had a vision which told him that the earth was going to roll up--purifying itself--and only the Indians would survive. Hearing this, I remembered the D/Lakota story that says the beginning of a new age would start when the buffalo which holds the waters back loses all its legs. Then the water will rush in and a new age will start. The Hindus, as previously mentioned, have a corresponding belief that mankind is approaching the beginning of a new cycle.

A member of the Ojibway Sun Bear Clan made a prophecy that the new age would start when mankind builds a house in the sky. Modern man, hearing this prophecy, laughed--but now, NASA is planning on building a space station. Is this the house in the sky that was referred to in the Sun Bear prophecy?

The voice of the collective unconscious, speaking through Edgar Cayce, prophesied that Planet Earth would experience a shift in its magnetic field, causing the planet to tilt. The time for this polar shift is very close to the beginning of the twenty-first century. This prophecy is almost identical to the Hopi prophecy. Astrologers also predict the end of a cycle in the year 2000. Coincidental? Or synchronistic?

In *Strangers Among Us: Enlightened Beings from a World to Come*, Ruth Montgomery stated that the UFO cosmonauts that have been appearing around the planet in recent years claim that the reason they're here in great numbers now is because of the polar shift. They say it's much like when there's an eclipse of the sun, mankind on earth comes out of their dwellings to witness it. Likewise, the polar shift has created enormous interest among many people throughout the universe. The cosmonauts have come to study this phenomenon and help the people of Planet Earth.

Scientists have estimated that the earth has gone through many previous polar shifts. A few scientists theorize that the last shift caused the instant freezing of the woolly mammoths that have been found in Siberia and Alaska.

The Hopis say they will be able to tell the beginning of the final stage of the purification when a Hopi kachina takes his mask off during a dance, revealing his identity.

Ruth Montgomery, receiving information via automatic writing, said that her guides told her that not everybody will want to live through the purification. Those who do, however should be encouraged to follow their own inner guidance. They will be intuitively led to safe places to survive the purification.

When God destroyed the last age with the great flood, He gave Noah a sign of the rainbow which symbolized that He would never totally destroy the world again. I see this sign as a reference to the safe places that were described in Ruth Montgomery's material.

The New Age is identified as the millenium of which the Bible speaks, according to Montgomery. "In the New Age," she said, "all of mankind will be brothers, without regard to race, sex, or creed." She further delineated that in the next age, the learning process will be speeded up. Books will be read almost at a glance, and the material contained within will be absorbed through mental osmosis. Our school systems will be changed dramatically. A person will be able to get the information he needs by tapping directly into the minds of others rather than by attending school for twelve years.

A Seneca legend states that there are seven worlds or seven ages that mankind on earth must evolve through. At the end of the fourth world, for example, we only move into the next age. When I read this, I remembered "Okawige," the traditional D/Lakota philosophy that all things move in cycles: that the beginning is the end, and the end is the beginning. This saying is almost exactly like the passage from the Bible: "I am the Alpha and the Omega, the beginning and the ending, saith the Lord, which is, and which was, and which is to come, the Almighty."

Jung said that modern man is looking outside for salvation when he should be looking inside. I wondered if this purification that so many cultures address is actually inside rather than outside. Cayce remarked in one of his psychic readings that Armageddon will be fought in the spirit world. The spirit world, to me, is the collective unconscious.

The book *The Jupiter Effect* by John Gribbin and Steven Plagueman predicted catastrophic events that were to happen in 1983. Many people viewed this as an indication of the end of the world. When 1983 arrived, nothing happened. The Aztec calendar foretold the end of the age as August 16, 1987. Many people felt that this was the end of the world. Yet August 16, 1987 came and went and there was no worldwide catastrophe. My question: "Is the purification an event that happens within the psyche?"

STRATEGIES FOR GLOBAL HARMONY

Being a man of reason (left brain functioning), I couldn't help but wonder if it wasn't synchronistic for so many different sources to say the same thing about the end of an age. Therefore, I decided to prepare for a natural catastrophe of global proportions. If it happens, I'll be ready, and if it doesn't, I'll be a better person for having prepared for the worst.

I would like to share some survival strategies which I discovered as a result of my experiences. During Christmas time 1982 I was living in Denver when a blizzard hit the city, dumping 35 inches of snow in twenty-four hours. The city was completely paralyzed. Thousands of holiday travelers were stranded at the airport, the train station, and the bus depot. The following morning I shoveled my way out of the parking lot, put on my tire chains, and went for a drive in West Denver. To my surprise, I found only four other vehicles moving on West Colfax Avenue. The sky was clearing, and people were beginning to move about. My brother Ken (who was visiting over the holidays) and I continued down Colfax Avenue, helping stalled motorists. We decided to get coffee and donuts to warm ourselves. But all the stores were closed. Eventually, we found one open. Entering the store, we encountered another surprise: almost all the food shelves were empty!

Later as we went on helping people dig out of the blizzard, I observed a sense of brotherhood among the people who helped each other. Months afterwards, looking at a photo journal of the storm, I recalled that Montgomery said we will all be brothers and sisters after the polar shift.

A thought came to me. If the shelves in the stores were empty for an extended period of time, where would we get our food? What would we do for medicine? During my youth, I remember my parents gathering herbs, plants, and wild fruits which they said could be used as food and medicine. But I didn't pay any attention to what they said at that time.

Having recently become more interested in natural foods and medicine, I detected an awareness occurring, which is termed wholistic health. I bought a book on healing herbs and, to my amazement, a majority of those listed were herbs used by the American Indians prior to the arrival of the Europeans. (Many traditional medicine men still use herbs to aid in the healing process.) I have started a collection of natural foods and herbs which I have harvested from the local area. My sister-in-law Janet who belongs to a fundamentalist Christian church reminded me that the Bible is an excellent resource on natural foods.

I feel that the knowledge of natural foods and medicines, along with the ability to grow your own food, would be helpful during natural catastrophes of any length. Understanding whole-mind thought would also be helpful for any individual who chooses to prepare for a worldwide natural catastrophe. Dr. Jung asserted that the information from the collective unconscious is just as valid as that from the conscious. Such knowledge can be understood if modern man deciphers the symbolic language of the unconscious.

To accomplish this, I would recommend becoming thoroughly familiar with American Indian philosophy and thought; studying the Edgar Cayce readings; using meditative techniques; and practicing listening to your inner voice. By listening to the inner self and following one's instincts and intuitions, a person may be guided to safety.

Several Native American holy people, as well, have told me that the spirits will help guide people who request their assistance. The Hopi say that only those clans who have retained their ceremonies will survive. Dawson No Horse urged the D/Lakota people to always retain and perform the Sun Dance.

As discussed in, "The Flowering Tree," Edgar Cayce stated that if one practiced brotherly love, peace, patience, balance and harmony, and had the ability to endure long-suffering situations for a period of two years, he would achieve a condition of wholeness with every thing. Having arrived at this state, one's spirit has completed its evolutionary journey on earth, and the individual would not be required to reincarnate. To develop this series of characteristics, I feel, would be an excellent way to escape any possible natural catastrophe.

Preparing for wholeness can also be accomplished through creating self-awareness. To review, Jung remarked that in order to achieve transcendent function (wholeness), one needed to complete individuation (self-awareness), which can be done by recognizing brain hemisphericy functions. A student learning through a whole-brain approach would become more cognizant of his own actions by relating them to hemispheric dominance.

Astrology is yet another way to aid oneself in attaining wholeness. Astrology, as previously mentioned, provides a mirror in which a person can recognize his easy and difficult aspects. By working on correcting one's negative personal traits, he is able to transcend his birth chart and achieve a state of wholeness.

Carl Jung declared that once an individual has actualized wholeness or oneness with everything, he or she would recognize this achievement by having a dream of a mandala. Dawson No Horse's altar held a mandala shaped like a six-pointed star. He said he had received this symbol of wholeness in a dream. To me, Dawson's altar symbol was evidence that he had completed his evolution on earth. Further testimony came when the spirits brought him through the wall after a vision quest, illustrating his ability to move from one dimension into another and back again. In considering this particular feat, I was curious about whether it might be what the Bible meant when describing the Rapture, which is explained as being physically lifted up to be with Christ. The Wakinyan Oyate had carried Dawson through the wall. (I feel the "Wakinyan Oyate" is a cultural linguistic name for the Christ spirit.) The capability of moving between dimensions, then, would be another way of escaping possible catastrophe.

One could also enlist the support of UFO cosmonauts. I myself have never seen a UFO, nor do I place too much hope in ever seeing one. If one does appear, however, I'm not going to shoot at it because the beings on it may simply be trying to communicate with me.

There may be people who are unable to practice any of the suggested methods for averting a catastrophe. According to Raymond Moody, though, they need not worry about death because there *is* life after life. Another way to deal with the catastrophe possibility is to understand the philosophy of reincarnation, which teaches that the consequences of this life are seen as the evolutionary growth of each soul and that each person has the free will to attain wholeness or prepare for the next life.

The law of karma, as a preparation for the next life, can be useful: if one is good to people, then goodness will return to you in your next life. Likewise, the negative qualities will return as well. Cayce said that this concept appears in the Bible as, "Vengeance is mine, saith the Lord." There are those who cannot accept what I have written, which is all right because I do not ask everyone to believe me. Cayce, however, stated that each person will eventually complete their evolution on earth whether they believe in karma or not. He commented that in each life, the soul gains through experience and that it takes an average of thirty lives for soul to reach wholeness.

The final technique I share for escape from catastrophe lies in traditional Native American belief. In the concept of Mitakuye Oyasin (everything is related) and the practice of traditional ceremonies for balance (Red Road), one would learn to accept the duality of every thing in the universe. It is this double nature or "The [Hopi] Twins" that holds the planet in balance. Today, though, Planet Earth is surrounded with negative brain wave energy which has created an imbalance. "The Twins" are getting weaker as they hold the planet in balance.

182

Ruth Montgomery related that her guides told her a planetary shift was inevitable. But I believe in the power of the ceremonies and in the power of prayer. I wonder, therefore, that if we can get enough of the earth's population to send good, positive, peaceful thought energy out into our solar system and to the sun, can we prevent a polar shift of Planet Earth? I recall attending a Spiritual Frontiers Fellowship meeting in Minneapolis in which the participants closed the meeting in meditation, then sent healing prayers to the sun! I contemplated, "Could a worldwide effort, a 'Planetary Sun Dance' be organized to bring balance back into mankind's life?"

D/LAKOTA PHILOSOPHY AND CEREMONY

Having presented the research in this book, I will now state the philosophy of the traditional D/Lakota as I perceive it.

First, the nature of the universe can be described as a whole which is symbolized by the circle. This philosophy can be described further by a review of the structure of the Lakota words used in the creation story.

Inyan - literal translation: "the creator." In=inner and yan=beginning or inner beginning.

Wakinyan - literal translation: "lightning or thunder beings." Wakinyan was Inyan's first creation. Wak, short for Wakan=spiritual, inyan=creator or spiritual creator.

Maka - literal translation: "the earth." (or my roots.) Ma=mine, ka=roots (Ella Deloria stated that in some instances the "ka" sound is substituted for "ca" or roots.) or my roots.

Mini - literal translation: "water." Mi=me, ni=spiritual quality of life or my spiritual quality of life.

Skan - literal translation: "spiritual power of the universe." ska=white or white spirit, n=nasal "n" or spiritual connotation.

Wi - literal translation: "the sun." (Ella Deloria states that "Wi" was a pre-Christian Lakota word for Great Spirit.) Wi=spiritual power.

Tate - literal translation: "the wind." Ta=physical form, te-physical form. (Traditional Lakota believe that to feel the wind was the ability to touch the invisible or spirits.) or physical form of the spirits.

Hanhepiwi - literal translation: "the night sun or moon." Han=it is said, hepi=third born, wi=spiritual power or spiritual power which was born third in line.

Pte - literal translation: "female buffalo." P or Pe=top of head, te=physical form (Traditional Lakota believe that the top of the head is where the spirit enters the body.) or place where spirit entered physical form.

A Lakota man's place within the universe can be described by reviewing the structure for the word man, "wicasa."

Wicasa - literal translation: "man." Wi=spiritual power, ca=roots, sa=red (Traditional Lakota believe they came from the red earth.) or man was of the spirit and his roots were red.

Winyan - literal translation: "woman." Wi=spirit power, inyan=creator (Traditional Lakota believe that the woman has the power of the creator.) or spirit with power of the creator.

The definitions above appeared in the paper entitled "A Compendium of Thoughts" by Dr. Donald Ross.)

D/Lakota philosophy states that everything was in pairs of opposites: good and bad, light and dark. To have one without the other would cause an imbalance. So they were given ceremonies to maintain a balance. In the ceremonies one would suffer (bad) so he could have his prayers answered (good). Traditional D/Lakota belief was that man's purpose on earth was to return to the center, and the method for doing this was to walk the Red Road (maintain a balanced life).

The date and place for the religious ceremonies was determined by the position of the White Buffalo Star Constellation.

The essential nature of God in the traditional D/Lakota culture is that the Great Spirit is the creator of all things and also that this creator is part of all things created.

Destiny, in traditional D/Lakota culture was contained in the belief that each person had a purpose or plan for his existence in this life. It was his duty to go on a vision quest to find out what that purpose was. Free will was when the parents allowed children to discover answers for themselves. The child was never told how to do a task, he was shown the task and then allowed to attempt it himself. This philosophy was practiced throughout D/Lakota culture, education, hunting, religion--all of life, in fact.

In traditional D/Lakota culture the people believed that a spirit entered the body at birth. So a ceremony was held to ask the Great Mystery that a good spirit enter the body. When the person died, his spirit went up to the Milky Way, then proceeded south. At the south end of the Milky Way an old lady who sat at a fork in the Milky Way and judged you by how you lived your life on earth. If you walked the Red Road or were generous, helped others and lived in harmony with all things, then she allowed you to take the left road which led you back to the center. If you lived your life on earth by walking the Black Road or being greedy and selfish, then she took you down the short path on the right and pushed you off. You then descended to earth and were reborn in a new body. This was to allow you another chance to live in harmony with all things. If a person died at an early age and did not have that opportunity, then an elder was selected to keep the soul/spirit for one year. During this time the elder would pray each day for the spirit to walk the Red Road, thus affording the youth's spirit an opportunity to take the long road on the left--back to the center or to finish his evolutionary journey on earth.

The traditional view of the D/Lakota man's relationship with the nation was spiritual in nature. The original nation consisted of seven tribes whose spiritual origins were from Wicahpi Sakowin (seven stars or the Pleiades). The original seven tribes were known as Oceti Sakowin (seven campfires). Individual tribes were called:

Mdewakantonwan (spirit water dwellers)
Sissetonwan (fish scale dwellers)
Wahpetonwan (camp among the leaves)
Wahpekute (shoot through the leaves dwellers)
Ihanktonwan (end dwellers)
Ihankonwana (little end dwellers)
Titonwan (prairie dwellers)
The structure of each tribe consisted of the following:

Itancan - chief. The Itancan was elected by the Ominiciye (council). The qualifications for Itancan were bravery, fortitude, generosity, and wisdom. It was also necessary to be a good husband, father, hunter, warrior, and—above all—a participator in the religious ceremonies. Achievement of these activities resulted in the awarding of an eagle feather. When 28 feathers were received, the person was entitled to wear the Eagle Feather Bonnet. A person wearing a bonnet with a trail indicated he had accomplished many deeds. The power of the Itancan was not absolute, but usually his decisions were unquestioned.

The Ominiciye (council) was made up of leaders from the civil societies. Qualifications for the council were: that one had to be a retired Akicita (warrior) officer, a retired hunter, a holy man or a former Itancan (chief). These men were the only Lakota allowed to wear the "fringed shirt." This shirt was a symbol of authority as well as of responsibility. The council met on issues of extreme importance to the entire tribe. Their decisions had to be unanimous, thus eliminating any split within the tribe. The larger tribes had an executive committee called Itancan Wicasa (chief men). This committee was elected by the council and usually had seven members. They had the power to overturn a chief's decision, but this was done only in rare occasions. Names for the civil societies were Owl Feather Headdress, White Horse Owners, Tall Ones, Buffalo Headdress, and Big Bellies.

The civil societies had membership qualifications similar to those of the Ominiciye. The Owl Feather Headdress Society had one particular spiritual qualification where the inductee had to carry a hot coal in his bare hand before he could become a member.

The Akicita (warrior) societies were the next rank in the tribal structure. Their duties were to police and protect the camp and to organize the buffalo hunts. Each summer the societies competed with each other in group dance contests. The society that won the contest earned the right to perform the Akicita duties for one year. The societies had names like Fox, Crow Owners, Brave Hearts, Badgers, and Grass Dance.

Besides being known for their warrior status, each society had additional skills. The Fox and Crow Owners also gained fame for their prowess as great hunters. The Badger and Grass Dance Societies were also known for their skill with medicine. The Brave Hearts were good/fair policemen. Each society elected twelve officers. The type of officer varied with each society, but usually they consisted of two pipe men, two drummers, four lance men, two rattle men, and two whippers. (Several societies also had whistle carriers, but the total number of officers was usually only 12 in number.) These officers had the responsibility of conducting the society duties and ceremonies.

The pipe men would begin each ceremony with a prayer. The drummers led the singers in singing society and honor songs. The rattle men led society dances and the whippers were the lead dancers. All society members and their spouses participated in the dances. The lance men administered the selection of people who were to be honored. These officers could be recognized by the "badge of honor" they wore or carried at the dances: pipe, rattle, whip, bustle, for instance. The type of badge (item) varied with each society. For example, the Grass Dance society had four officers who wore the dance bustle, and the Crow Owners society had only two officers who wore the "Crow belt" bustle. These were the only societies that used the bustle. Another example is the head roach was common to the Grass Dance and Brave Heart societies.

Another group of societies that had equal rank with the Akicita but who were non-military were the Hanble (dream) societies. These societies had such names as Elk, Bear, Buffalo, Thunder (Heyoka). Their purpose was to help people understand their dreams. The holy man of each dream society would, upon request, conduct a ceremony wherein the spirits would speak through him and interpret the requestor's dream. The dream society that a person belonged to was determined by the animal or object that appeared in their dream or vision. This dream or vision usually came on their first vision quest. A person's dream was shared with the people and the message was used to help guide the person, the tribe and the nation.

At the society ceremonies all dances were performed in a circle, with the dancers moving in a clockwise motion. Only the veterans and heyoka (thunder dreamers) were allowed to dance counter-clockwise. (The traditional D/Lakota felt that to shoot someone out of anger was not right. It was more honorable to touch your enemy than to kill him. But they also realized that each person had a plan for this life. Maybe in this life one was meant to be a soldier, so out of respect the veterans were honored by being allowed to dance counter- clockwise.)

The heyoka was a contrary; he intentionally did things back-wards. He served two purposes--first, he provided a balanced psychological perspective on all things by performing the op-posite. Second, his actions were viewed with laughter, thus af-fording a healing effect for the spectators.

The next group within the tribal structure was the Oyate (people). The people were divided into tiospaye (extended families/hunting and planting groups). The tiyospaye were originally matriarchal in order. The oldest woman was considered head of the home, but the senior man was the spokesman, so the two had to be in communication continually. There were no fami-ly names; each person had only one name. The common name they shared was their band or tribal name.

Tiyospaye members could become a member of an Akicita society by invitation only. The young people had to meet the fol-lowing qualifications before being invited to join: complete a vision quest, come from a respectable family or touch an enemy.

Education of the young was largely done through example and by allowing children to discover answers for themselves. A favorite teaching method was to tell a story with a good moral

189

value. Children were never given waste material to practice on. They were given the very best. In this way they would be encouraged to do their very best. The children were not disciplined if they could not accomplish the task. The instructor, usually a grandmother, grandfather, aunt or uncle, just took more time in working with the slow learners. Child discipline was not done by the parents. It was done by an aunt or uncle but only when necessary. This allowed the child to have a loving and open communication with the parents. A technique used in disciplining the younger ones was the use of an imaginary character (Cici man). This character was used to frighten the child into good behavior.

Education was primarily vocational, thus preparing the youngster for a productive place within the culture, such as planter, hunter, fisherman, dressmaker, arrow maker, cook.

Values--generosity, courage, fortitude, and wisdom--were taught by example to the children. Of these, the wisdom gained through personal experiences was held in highest regard, especially that acquired in the religious ceremonies. An old Lakota saying is that experience is the best teacher.

The holy people believed that the spirits influenced them to say or do certain things. They knew that the spirits existed in groups and that each group performed functions only for certain things. Some names for these groups are Wakinyan Oyate (Thunder People), Tatanka Oyate (Buffalo People), Wanblee Oyate (Eagle People), Sinte Sapa Oyate (Black Tail Deer People).

The traditional D/Lakota knew they were related to all things, and that the path of the Red Road would allow them to return to the seven stars. They also knew that they could do whatever they wanted, that they need not follow their dreams or visions if they so chose. But they understood, too, the consequences of not following their dreams or walking the Black Road.

Now let us experience a scenario from a traditional D/Lakota Akicita ceremony. The tribe has just arrived at a new campsite. The camp is arranged in a circle with an opening in the east to serve as the entrance. The circle permeates D/Lakota philosophy and thought because of the belief that all things operate in cycles. The entrance to the east symbolizes the direction from which Father Sun sends his power to all things on Mother Earth.

Upon completion of setting up the camp, the Akicita Society, which had won the right to perform the duties for the camp for that year, had their eyapaha (crier) tell everyone to come to the center of the camp circle to participate in a ceremony.

The ceremony begins with prayers by the pipe men officers. The drum officers then lead the drummers in the first song of the ceremony. It is during this song that the rattle carrier officers dance. At the conclusion of this set of songs, the rattle officers assign society members to camp guard duty, pony guard duty, wood gathering, latrine marking, and hunting duty.

The next set of society songs are sung and danced in the form of a procession around the camp circle. The lance officers who lead the procession and select people they wish to honor. This is done by placing a short lance/stick in the ground in front of the honored person's tipi. The dancers and singers then return to the center of the camp circle. The people selected are so honored that they bring gifts (food, clothes, robes, and horses) to give to the society. The society then conducts honor songs for these selected people; those chosen are held in high esteem. After the songs, the society calls certain people forward to receive the gifts which the honorees have donated. The people selected to receive the gifts are the old, the sick, the unfortunate, and the chief men. Each person who receives a gift thanks the honored person and gives a short speech, boasting about the talents and exploits of the honored person.

By participating in the give-away, the more one gives, the greater the chances are for advancement within the tribe/nation. So the economics of the D/Lakota have to do with giving to gain. At the conclusion of the give-away ceremony, everyone joins in on social dances.

191

When the dancing ceases, a great feast is given by the society. All are invited. After the meal, the dancing continues late into the night. Other occasions for Akicita give-away ceremonies were returning from a successful hunt or a successful battle. The non-military societies, the religious ceremonies, and the domestic ceremonies (births, marriages, deaths) also held give-away ceremonies. So the entire year was filled with the philosophy of "giving to gain." Thus, there were no orphanages, no nursing homes, no funeral parlors, no welfare, and no jails.

* * * * *

After I wrote the first part of this chapter--the philosophy part, the idea of including a scenario of a traditional ceremony came to me. When that part was finished, I felt the entire chapter seemed to close more naturally. Some time later, I realized that the scenario section and the concepts presented there--was the fulfilment to my very first vision.

It was the third day of that vision quest. An orange monarch butterfly appeared and sat right in front of me, moving its wings very gently. It flew away and then came back. It did this seven times. After its seventh return, it sat in front of me again, continuing to gently move its wings back and forth. I knew then it was a messenger.

Suddenly, it popped into my mind that it is necessary for the D/Lakota people to return to an acceptance of concepts of the traditional societies. It seems realistic that these concepts contained in a traditional D/Lakota way of life can also serve as an example for *all* people everywhere.

At first, I dismissed the appearance of the butterfly of my vision as not being of much import, thinking that others I knew who had gone on the hill had received such *wakan* visions as deer and buffalo. Its significance in my vision, as well as the connection to the scenario presented as the second part of this chapter became clear to me when I suddenly recalled an old D/Lakota legend.

At a time long ago when a particular camp was in chaos and the people seemed to be extremely disunified, a butterfly came and sat on a woman's shoulder. It whispered in her ear what was to be done to help the people. She then set out to bring harmony to the camp.

A JOURNEY FOR PEACE

A few days after being a presenter at a peace conference held during the Harmonic Convergence, I was surprised by an invitation to visit the NATO (North Atlantic Treaty Organization) headquarters in Brussels, Belgium. I immediately recognized this invitation as being synchronistic and that the trip pertained to world peace.

Dr. Yvonne Cheek, director of the Hubert Humphrey Institute of Public Affairs in Minneapolis, Minnesota had extended the invitation. When I asked her what was expected of me, she said that I was selected as a midwest opinion leader and that a short report would be sufficient. I accepted the invitation and began to prepare for the trip right away because it was scheduled for October 16-26, 1987, less than two months from the time I initially learned about it. This chapter is an edited version of my NATO report.

We left Minneapolis at 5:30 p.m. on October 16th and arrived in London, England at 7:30 a.m. the next morning. From there we trans ferred to a flight which took us to Brussels. The first few days at NATO I couldn't see how this trip could possibly pertain to peace. It wasn't until the evening of October 21st at Wassenaar, Holland--when I had a dream that helped me to realize what had been taking place during the first days of my NATO visit--that I understood. I will speak more about this dream later.

Upon arrival at the Burssels airport, I waited for our guide at the exit to the airport. When no one came, I asked a taxi driver how much it would cost to go to the Astoria Hotel. He told me it was 800 Belgian franks. I returned to the airport building and changed $50 into Belgian franks. The exchange bank gave me 1,800 franks, and I thus learned that the exchange rate was $1.00 = 36 Belgian franks. The taxi driver told me that the city was half French and half Flemish (Belgian). He also said that nowadays a lot of Africans (Moroccans) and Turks live in the city.

I checked into the hotel and met Mr. Steven Hintz of our group. He wanted to visit, but I was completely exhausted, so I went immediately to my room and fell asleep. When I awoke, I took a shower, then went for a walk. As I walked down a side street from the Rue Royale, I suddenly had a flashback. I was standing on a similar street in Germany 25 years earlier as a young soldier with the 505th paratroopers. This flashback was similar in definition to what one would see or feel in a vision quest. Being knowledgeable about the information within the personal unconscious part of the psyche and the methods in which this information penetrates consciousness, I was not alarmed by my experience.

I spent the rest of the day resting and sleeping. I had a hard time adjusting to the six-hour time change. Twelve noon in Brussels is 6:00 a.m. at home. My digestive system also experienced a change in food and liquid consumption. Very little water is consumed. I did not see any drinking water fountains in Europe, even at the airport. Bottled water is sold in the cafe in a bottle similar to a Coke bottle.

I found my room to be very small, but I had expected this. My bed was also very small and was similar to an Army bed in size. The bathtub was so narrow that if one were large, it would be difficult to fit into it. The shower was only shoulder high. The TV had 16 channels. I recognized the following languages on these channels: English, French, German, Spanish and Flemish.

I had brought two gifts from home to be given to whom I knew not. I just sensed that I had to bring them to Europe. The gifts were a feather bonnet and a rock from Harney Peak. I mentioned these gifts to Yvonne and told her I felt that they should be given from the group. But during the week, I didn't get a feeling for whom the gifts should be shared. I will comment later about what happened with these gifts.

As I walked the streets of Brussels, I noticed that there were no birds. I wondered about that. Later at an intersection, I saw a dead pigeon, just recently killed. I prayed for Wakan Tanka (God) to help his spirit on its evolutionary journey. Walking on, I came to a McDonald's hamburger shop. French fries and a Coke cost 68 Belgian franks.

Monday morning as I left the hotel, I observed how crowded the street was with people, the cars in a traffic jam. Auto fumes filled the air. Our group boarded the bus which took us to NATO, located on the outskirts of town.

NATO personnel briefed us all day about their organization. Their presentations were informational and well-rehearsed. It appeared they had done this type of program many times previously. It also appeared they were selling themselves, and I wondered for what reason. NATO interests? Personal interests? Or perhaps both?

A video-tape on the Third Dimension impressed me. It was about how NATO grants are helping NATO countries. The example given was about how the stained glass windows in the Cathedral at Cologne, Germany were marred so badly by acid rain that they were falling out. NATO gave the Germans a grant to develop a chemical spray to protect the windows. I thought about applying for a NATO grant to do a study on Traditional Native American Philosophy and Thought because I feel this philosophy contains an answer to the dilemma of modern man.

NATO presentor U.S. Colonel A.T. Springer's manner struck me as one who was genuinely interested in peace in the world.

At lunch I visited with a member of our group, Dr. Richard Green. As I was explaining to him the influence American Indians had on the U.S. Constitution, he said, "When are you going to stand up and tell the group about this?" I said nothing, for I felt like he wanted to "throw it in their face." That is not my style. Furthermore, the timing was not right. I will mention more about this later.

Tuesday I arose and packed my bags for the trip to Rotterdam. On the way there, the tour guide explained that the Rue Royale where our hotel was located was known as the King's Street, but it was in poor condition because the government didn't have enough money to fix it. Upon leaving the city, we saw the Atomium Structure and the Belgian Court. It was raining lightly now as we twisted and turned in the narrow streets of Old Belgium. On the outskirts of the city was a nuclear generating plant. The guide explained that there were seven nuclear plants in Belgium. The countryside in this area displayed mostly dairy cows.

Near the Holland border, a larger number of cultivated fields appeared. The country was still very green for this late in October. About 25 percent of the leaves on the trees had turned to autumn colors. The tour guide pointed out the large number of hothouses in Holland, boasting that Dutch people provide most of the fresh vegetables in Europe.

Once in Rotterdam, we had a new tour guide. She explained that the city was almost totally destroyed in World War II by the Germans and had to be rebuilt. I wondered if this was NATO propaganda. I had visited Rotterdam 25 years ago and heard the same story at that time by another tour guide.

It is now 40 years after the war. How much longer will people in this area continue punishing others for their mistakes? Or has the time arrived for us to begin realizing how we are all related?

After a great lunch, we retired to a small lecture room. Our speaker was a retired captain, J. J. Vaessen of the R.N.L. Navy. I very much liked his opening remarks about the five great Jews (Moses, Jesus, Marx, Freud, Einstein) because, to me, they once again portrayed how all things and all people are related. The rest of the captain's talk was a reinforcement of NATO ideals: Beware of the Russians.

On the way to our hotel which was very close to the North Sea Coast, our tour guide told us that there are only 800 windmills left and that they are all national monuments.

Coffee and cookies were served as we mixed with the host group. At my table was group member Lauren Soth and a retired Justice from the Netherlands Supreme Court. the Justice began talking about World War II. I told him that my dad was in Patton's army during the war but that I was a Vietnam era veteran. He sat up straight and had a surprised look on his face. It was like he realized a new generation of American had arrived. I listened to the speakers give their reasons for the existence of NATO and became very uneasy over the purpose of my presence on this trip. I felt it was meant to be a journey for peace, but I did not get this impression from the presentors. I awoke refreshed and immediately recalled a dream I'd had during the night. Being a student of Jungian psychology, I knew instantly that this was a message from the collective unconscious. Having interpreted dreams for the past eight years, I quickly began to analyze my dream.

In the major part of it, there was a Lakota family performing a ceremony, but they didn't understand the ceremony. They were only going through the motions. I understood this to mean that the family (NATO), when performing their ceremonies (informational presentations), were only going through the motions and no longer understood the meaning behind their efforts. Granted, the information put forth within the presentations is valid and a majority of it I had not known previously. Examples: There are sixteen countries in NATO with whom the U.S. has treaties. We have five treaties with other non-NATO nations around the world as well. The U.S. spends $200 billion on defense; $120 billion of that is spent on NATO. In addition, the military industrial complex has a tremendous influence on government spending. This is being done not only in the U.S., but in other countries as well. The bottom line message of NATO is that as long as there is NATO, a mutual assurance of destruction will prevail between east and west. The result is a stalemate, which they interpret as peace. I felt refreshed, though, because I believe the dream answered my questions about NATO. Incidentally, traditional D/Lakota culture utilized dream interpretations to guide the lives of the people.

About 9:00 on the morning of October 21, 1987 we departed Wassenaar for The Hague. The presentations there by the Netherlands Ministry of Defense staff were excellent because of their use of visual aids. Being an educator, I recognized this delivery technique as a wholistic (whole brain) approach. A current trend in education, preceded by statistics identifying our nation's youth as needing a more whole-brain type of instruction in order to more fully understand information being presented, is a move in this direction.

A tasty lunch was served at an Indonesian restaurant. From my previous trips to the Netherlands, I knew there was an Indonesian population there, but I didn't realize the great number of Africans now living in Holland. It was explained by the tour guide that the social system of the Netherlands and Belgium led to the migrations of foreign nationalists into their countries. I found these comments to be propagandistic. Those who study world history know that the Dutch and Belgian nations conquered many countries and exported resources to their home country. I felt it was only fair for the conquered people to be able to migrate to the conquerer nation and to be able to benefit from the natural resources which originally came from their home country.

In the afternoon we attended a counter-terrorist exercise put on by the Royal Netherland Marines, a demonstration which made a strong impression on me. After a short lecture, we were asked to volunteer for the demonstration. I quickly raised my hand but was not selected. Seeing the demonstration rather than being a participant in it, however, allowed me to view it more fully and clearly. As we came outside to watch the demonstration, the first thing I noticed was that the armored personnel carriers that had been parked on the field when we came in were no longer there. Looking around, I saw riflemen positioned as snipers.

Suddenly, two shots split the air. Two terrorists came out with a pair of hostages. After a brief moment, five more hostages were brought out by two more terrorists. Total--seven hostages and four terrorists. The terrorists loaded the hostages onto a bus. The counter-terrorists, using the element of surprise, attacked with machine-gun fire and exploding grenades. The armored personnel carriers advanced from four directions toward the bus. One carrier bumped the front of the bus, knocking the hostages and terrorists about. Simultaneously, the other carriers pulled alongside and the counter-terrorist squad attacked by crashing through the bus windows and through the doors.

The whole demonstration was completed in approximately 30 to 40 seconds. Afterwards, we were allowed to talk to the counter-terrorist squad. The young man I talked to was 24 years old. He wore an armor plate vest and his weapon was an MP-5 machine gun with two magazines, each holding approximately 32 bullets. The weapon could be fired with both eyes open, thus enhancing the speed of an attack.

After this demonstration, I made a one day stop in Amsterdam. I quickly visited the Van Gogh Museum and returned to my hotel where I had a noon luncheon with Mr. Govert DeGroot, a man with the workshop of Indigenous Peoples. He began our meeting by telling me about the injustices which were happening to indigenous people around the planet. I felt sad hearing this, but I also believe in "okawige" (karma). I told him that if I were invited to lecture in Amsterdam, my approach would be a positive one and that I would work for unity and harmony. I also explained my research on the ozone layer and its connection to brain waves. He accepted my philosophy and stated that they their group would like to invite me to lecture.

That evening we had dinner with a group of "real people" of Brussels. My place was between a woman named Eva Geist from Germany on my left and a countess, Dominique Von DeWerve De Vorsselaer from Brussels on my right. Our hostess, Dr. Reba Curruth, told me that the countess was very interested in Native American history and culture and had asked specifically to be seated where she could visit with me. I found the discussions by the Europeans interesting because the French and Belgian were passive, while the German was forward.

I felt that the dinner discussion on NATO was informative, but a majority of the group agreed that a much greater danger threatens mankind. The cover story in the October 19, 1987 issue of *Time* addresses this threat. There are many scientific reports on the diminishing ozone layer. NOVA, on Public TV, has a one-hour special on the topic. But the *Time* article is the first in which this information has reached the public in layman's terms. In personal research on this topic, I found that many Native American ceremonies can be performed to decrease and/or even eliminate the destruction of the ozone layer. Earlier, I had asked a NATO staff person if anything was being done in the area of a scientific study of psychic phenomenon. He said, "No, nothing at all," and he gave me a puzzled look. Apparently, my personal life is so involved with Native American ceremonies (psychic phenomenon) that I sometimes forget that others have no idea what I'm talking about.

The following morning we were briefed by NATO presentor Colonel Elmar Dinter from the German military. After the briefing, I discussed with him the idea of getting the two Germanies reunited. He said, "What do you mean?" I told him that the two most powerful nations on earth have been influenced by Native American philosophy and thought. The U.S. Constitution was heavily influenced by the government of the Iroquois Confederacy. In fact, James Madison studied the Confederacy for approximately ten years before writing the U.S. Constitution. Ben Franklin also spoke in favor of the Iroquois government during a Continental Congress meeting. On the other hand, the U.S.S.R.'s Communist philosophy of Marx was strongly influenced by early writings about Native Americans. The book *Ancient Society* by Henry Lewis Morgan is considered a classic by Marxists.

I feel that the ideologies of the U.S. and the U.S.S.R. are polarizations of one type of government that, together, could work for both countries, as described earlier in this chapter and also in "D/Lakota Philosophy and Ceremony." The two need to work in harmony or become integrated in order to function properly. Has this occurred in Japan? Many of the Japanese auto and high-tech companies are people-oriented. (communal?) Now this idea appears to have spread to the U.S. Today workers sometimes buy out a company because it's going under; then it becomes the people's company (profit-sharing or people's capitalism?) Eight thousand companies in the U.S. are currently using this approach, Pan American Airlines and Avis Car Rental being two of the largest. But this idea did not originate in Japan; it was introduced to them by General MacArthur when he was rebuilding Japan after the war. Some believe he received the idea at West Point when he was studying military history of the American Indian. But the American Indians were not the originators of the idea because they received their information in the ceremonies.

Japan is taking the lead for the capitalist countries in utilizing a more cooperative (balanced) approach in economics. Another Asian country, China, is the leading Communist country for a more cooperative (balanced) approach in economics. China now allows private enterprise an equal chance with communal efforts for its people.

Germany represents satellites of the two super powers. If they could be reunited as a cooperative (profit sharing) entity, maybe the two super powers would start moving toward a reduction of tensions. Currently Germany is anxiously watching Poland to see if the Russians allow Poland to become a cooperative. I am not a student of nationalistic ideologies, but I think a cooperative approach is almost identical to socialist thought. Is socialism the blend of democracy and communism that Germany needs? Both extremes have their ills and both appear to be at the point of reconstruction.

Traditional Native American ideology contained both democratic and communal thought. It was a system that worked.

Could it be possible that traditional Native American philosophy and thought contains an answer for modern man? Colonel Dinter has asked me to send him the information on this subject. He was very interested in this topic.

The final briefing of NATO was by Ambassador Guy de Muyser from Luxembourg. De Muyser gave an explanation of the Russian psyche which I easily understood because of my studies in brain hemisphericy. My immediate thought was that I wished I could give a presentation on brain hemisphericy to influential people in the governments of the world. Maybe this would be the spark needed to start dialogue toward world harmony.

I had an opportunity to visit de Muyser after his presentation. During our chat, he told me he was in Moscow when Marine Sergeant Lonetree was there. He said he had an opportunity to meet Sergeant Lonetree. He seemed genuinely pleased to know the sergeant. The idea that Lonetree was found guilty of espionage by the Marine Corps seemed to escape him. He was very receptive to me and extremely interested in Native American history and culture. I told him the same story I had told Colonel Dinter. Ambassador de Muyser said, "Please send me more information on that topic." He told me he wanted to review it so he would be able to respond to it. Before departing, he asked again that I send him information, giving me his home address and telephone number.

Later, in talking to group member Mr. Nick Johnson, he told me he thought that in order for mankind to survive on this planet, we needed to adopt a philosophy similar to the traditional Native Americans. He shocked me further by stating that he believed that mental telepathy would be the language of the future. I have great respect for Mr. Johnson and hold his opinion in high regard.

That morning on the bus I had the good fortune to ride beside Ms. Elizabeth Williams. We discussed our home lives in South Dakota and our experiences in Amsterdam (she had visited there years before). She asked me what I thought about the Bradley

Bill in Congress, which asks for the return of the sacred Black Hills to the Sioux Nation. I said I agree with the Indians who believe the Black Hills are sacred, but I have a feeling that the Bradley Bill may not be the answer.

We concluded our group discussions as NATO opinion leaders with the idea that each would write about his experiences only if he so desired.

Upon returning to the hotel, I prepared for a trip to Germany the next day. My German contact in Austria couldn't make the meeting, but I decided to go to Mainz, Germany since that is where I had lived for three years. I left Brussels at noon after some last-minute shopping for my family. When I reached the German border via train, the border guards/customs agents boarded the train to review passports of individuals entering Germany. I prepared for a stern, disciplined, almost military-type border guard to question me, this being my experience of 25 years ago. To my surprise, the customs agent was very cordial, relaxed and friendly. He made me feel welcome in Germany.

I arrived in Mainz late that afternoon on October 24, 1987. I went to the front gate of Lee Barracks. Standing there, many memories rushed into my head. I went to look for my old watering holes but found them all gone. I met two young GI's and had a short visit with them. I told them I had lived there 25 years before. They both told me that they had not yet been born when I was stationed in Mainz. I was suddenly and abruptly reminded of how old I am, and I wondered, "Where did all the years go?" As I walked around the city, it appeared as a faint shadow of the Germany I remembered. Only a small portion of the city had been retained as a historical section. The Oberbayern no longer had a Bavarian band. The music was by a rock- and-roll group from the Philippines. The Germans were fascinated with my long hair, looking upon it in favor. This made me feel good and I was glad that I hadn't cut off my hair as I had planned for this European trip. My wife had told me to be proud of who I was and that I didn't have to apologize to anyone by cutting off my hair.

I was up early and finished my photography route. I then caught the late morning train back to Brussels so I could keep my appointment with a French professor that afternoon. As I left Germany, I wondered if I would ever return. I was comforted by the fact that my contact said he knew of a German publisher in Hamburg who was extremely interested in setting up a lecture tour for me for the following year.

Professor Didier Dupont from Hellemmes-Lille, France arrived exactly on schedule. We visited for three hours. He was teaching himself the Lakota language and wanted to know the proper way to pronounce Lakota words. He audio-taped our entire conversation. Professor Dupont was extremely knowledgeable about the Lakota people and had presented many lectures on traditional Lakota philosophy and thought throughout Europe.

I knew immediately it was he who was to receive the wapaha (feather headdress). I explained that it was worn as a persona (Jungian concept that allows the collective psyche to speak). It was worn at peace meetings as well as in battle, for it was considered more honorable to touch your enemy than to kill him. I presented the headdress to him as a teaching aid because I felt it would help him explain our traditional knowledge. Professor Dupont felt so honored upon receiving this gift that he wanted to cry. I could not look at him, for I knew if he cried, I would too. Before we said goodbye, I gave him another gift. It was a rock I had gotten from on top of Harney Peak in the Black Hills. I told him this rock was sacred because the Black Hills are sacred and that the Black Hills are sacred because Mother Earth is sacred. He nodded his head, indicating he understood. At that moment, Professor Dupont then shared with me the fact that he was given the task of preparing testimony on the Black Hills which would be given to the French representative of the United Nations for presentation at the United Nations. He was glad to receive my opinion about the Black Hills and said he would work on setting up a lecture for me in France. The purpose of the lecture would be to equip the French representative with a back ground on the sacredness of the Black Hills. At last I felt that the peace mission of my trip was fulfilled. Synchronistically, I had met with Professor Dupont on October 25, 1987, the same date as my 47th birthday.

I wrote this report aboard a 747 jet headed back to Minneapolis, Minnesota and then on to Bismarck, North Dakota. Thinking about returning home to the Standing Rock Reservation, I remembered the story about how we got that name. Long ago the people were in camp at this place. They decided to move the camp to a new location. Upon setting up the new camp, they discovered that a woman and her baby were missing. They hurriedly returned to this site to look for her. They found her but to their amazement, they discovered that she and her baby had turned to stone. The story ends there, but I feel it is incomplete. The original ending is lost in antiquity. What remains, I feel, is allegorical with an esoteric meaning. The allegory is that people are related to the rocks, and the hidden meaning is that the Standing Rock is alive, only waiting to be rediscovered. We now know that all things contain atoms and, depending upon the vibratory frequencies of these atoms, the determination of solid, liquid, or gas is made.

Early during the week one of the other tour participants had asked me, "How do you retain your original beliefs in this modern industrialized society?" I responded by saying that in my search for my roots/identity, I discovered that traditional Native American ceremonies closely tied into the discipline of astrology. In studying astrology, I learned about a concept that was identical to the Jungian concept of synchronicity. In the astrological teachings, it is said that the situations which exist today are the result of the positions of celestial bodies. Cayce commented that the solar systems were created for man, these situations thus affording each of us the opportunity to balance our karma, if we so desire. The

206

best way to balance our karma is by helping those people/nations with problems that are identical to our own. If you're an alcoholic, for instance, help an alcoholic. If you are a handicapped person, help another handicapped individual. If you are prejudiced, help others to see the error of their ways. These are only suggestions; you don't have to do any of them. As a matter of fact, you need not believe what I speak about. I only share it because it is my answer to surviving in these modern times. The old people say, "Learn from your mistakes." So I try to accept everything for what it is and to make the best of each situation one day at a time.

EPILOGUE

When I told Dawson No Horse the dream I received on my first vision quest, he responded by asking me to study it; not to grab it and run, but to study it. This was Dawson's method of teaching, by permitting individuals to discover answers for themselves and by setting an example. I have gained a tremendous amount of wisdom from two people who have used this way of teaching--Dawson and my father Harvey Ross (born at Keyapaha, Rosebud Reservation, South Dakota on March 10, 1919.) I was also highly influenced as an educator by my mother, Agnes Allen Ross, also an educator. In that vein, I have tried to write this book in an informative manner, allowing the reader the free will to discover his or her own answers.

In preparing this manuscript for publication, I asked an acquaintance to type my work as I verbally restructured each sentence. The following middle section of this epilogue is a short piece I requested that she share.

* * * * *

My name is Jean Katus. I formerly taught English at Standing Rock College in Ft. Yates, North Dakota. In August 1987 shortly after I returned from the Denver "Mitakuye Oyasin" conference at Harmonic Convergence time, which Chuck Ross had organized and in which he had presented his lectures series, he asked me if I would be interested in transcripting a manuscript of the lectures. I readily agreed.

For about four nights before we began the work, I was awakened around 4:00 a.m. by strange dreams that I couldn't recall in the morning. Then around 2:30 a.m. on the morning of the day we were to start the work, I had a very vivid dream. Feeling it was significant, I told myself before falling back to sleep that I would remember it in the morning. Upon awakening, the dream came back to me in full. Though another person was the central figure in the dream, I knew that it wasn't he but Chuck that the dream was about. The details made little sense to me and left me agitated all day, but I was so busy that I didn't have much time to reflect on it.

As the time grew closer for Chuck to come to my house so we could begin working on the manuscript, my agitation increased. In an effort to allay my anxiety, I telephoned my sister Delaine who lives in St. Louis and sometimes uses a pendulum for assistance in problem solving. What she picked up from her pendulum, after clearing herself and asking me to do the same, was that I had nothing to be concerned about but that there was a very powerful "presence" in my house at that moment--one so strong she could "feel" it all the way from North Dakota to Missouri! I said, "It's Dawson!" Almost before I got the words out of my mouth, Delaine's pendulum started swinging so wildly in a "yes" answer that she could hardly hold onto it, and her hands became very cold. She told me to calm myself by smudging with cedar, which I did.

When Chuck arrived, the agitation was gone. The work went well that first night, and it wasn't until the next session that I told him about the dream I'd had. I felt sure that Dawson's spirit had been "checking things out" for the four nights before we had begun the project. My sister's pendulum confirmed that such a spirit had, most certainly, "visited" my house. After hearing about the incident, Chuck said that at our previous session he had felt that the spirits were helping him "find the right words" as he restructured the lecture manuscript into written form. He determined that a visit by Dawson's spirit was a positive indication that the project was meant to be.

The entire experience, for me, was a graphic illustration that we are, indeed, all related!

*   *   *   *   *

In January of 1982, Dawson was on his deathbed at Fitzsimmons Army Hospital in Denver, Colorado. I was living in Denver at that time, so I had the good fortune of being able to call on him frequently. On another occasion when I went to visit him, I found a woman whom I did not know caring for him. Dawson must have seen a question in my facial expression because he said, "Her baby was healed in one of my ceremonies, and she wants to help me now that I'm in need."

I was immediately reminded of the Biblical story about how Jesus healed Mary Magdalene and from that moment on, she constantly cared for him. The story continues that once while she was washing his feet, the disciples became jealous and claimed he loved her more than he did them. He admonished them by replying that he loved everyone equally.

Dawson passed away on January 28, 1982. Hundreds of people from different cultures and denominations paid their respects at his funeral. One of his last requests was *Okiciyapo*, "Help each other."

That is one of the reasons for the writing of this book.

Ho Hecatu Yelo
"That's the way it is"

Mitakuye Oyasin
"We are all related"

BIBLIOGRAPHY

Alexander, George. "How Life on Earth Began" (printed in *Americans Before Columbus*). Reader's Digest. August, 1985.

Beasley, Victor. *Your Electro-Vibratory Body.* University of the Trees, 1970.

Berlitz, Charles. *The Mystery of Atlantis.* Avon, 1976.

Berner, Jeff. *The Holography Book.* Avon Books, 1980.

Blakeslee, Thomas R. *The Right Brain.* Anchor Press/Doubleday, 1980.

Blanchard, David. *Seven Generations.* Center for Curriculum Development, Kahnawake Survival School, 1980.

Book of Mormon.

Brown, Joseph Epes. *The Sacred Pipe.* Penguin Books, 1971.

Campbell, Joseph. *The Masks of God, Oriental Mythology.* Penguin Books, 1976.

Campbell, Joseph, editor. *The Portable Jung.* Penguin, 1976.

Capra, Fritjof. *The Tao of Physics.* Shambhala, 1975.

Cavendish, Richard, editor. *Man, Myth, and Magic.* Marshall Cavendish, 1983.

Cayce, Edgar Evans. *Edgar Cayce on Atlantis.* Warner Books, 1968.

Charroux, Robert. *The Mysteries of the Andes.* Avon Books, 1974.

Circle of Unity (proclamation to the Native Americans from the Baha'i Faith). Baha'i Publishing Trust, 1980.

Coffer, William E. *Spirits of the Sacred Mountains.* Van Nostrand Reinhold Co., 1978.

Cousins, Norman. *Anatomy of an Illness as Perceived by the Patient.* Bantam, 1981.

"Covenant," Vol. 2, No. 2, Lesson XIV: Holistic Healing. Association for Research and Enlightenment, Inc., 1980.

Deloria, Ella. *Speaking of Indians.* Dakota Press, 1979.

Elders, Lee J. and Thomas K. Welch. *UFO...Contact from the Pleiades.* Genesis III Publishing, 1979.

Erdoes, Richard (editor). *Lame Deer, Seeker of Visions.* Pocket Books, 1976.

Fell, Barry. *America B.C.* Pocket Books, Inc., 1979

Ferguson, Marilyn. *The Aquarian Conspiracy.* J.P. Tharcher, 1980.

Forrest, Steven. "Astrology and the Bible" (printed in *Welcome to Planet Earth,* Virgo Issue, Vol. 6, No. 3). Welcome to Planet Earth, 1986.

Gammon, Margaret H. *Astrology and the Edgar Cayce Readings.* A.R.E. Press, 1967.

Goodman, Ronald. "Lakota Star Knowledge and the Black Hills." Sinte Gleska College, 1983.

Graham, F. Lanier. *The Rainbow Book.* Shambhala Publications, 1975.

Gribbin, John and Steven Plagueman. *The Jupiter Effect.* Vintage Books, 1976.

Hall, Calvin S. and Gardner Lindzey. *Theories of Personality.* John Riley & Sons, 1978.

Hassrick, Royal. *The Sioux.* University of Oklahoma Press, 1964.

Hills, Dr. Christopher. *Supersensonics: The Science of Radiational Paraphysics.* University of the Trees, 1978.

Hitching, Francis. *The Mysterious World.* Holt, Rinehard & Winston, 1979.

Hurlburt, Sid. "A Pagan Tradition has Taken over Christmas," *USA Today,* December 11, 1987.

Jacobs, Don. "Astrology's Pew in Church," *Astrology Now,* 1978.

Jung, Carl Gustav. *Flying Saucers.* Princeton University Press, 1978.

_____. *Man and His Symbols.* Doubleday, 1969.

_____. *Memories, Dreams, Reflections*. Pantheon, 1963.

Katus, Jean. Testimonial, 1988.

Kondratov, Alexander. *The Riddles of Three Oceans*. Imported Publications, 1974.

Krajenke, Robert. *A Million Years to the Promised Land*. A Bantam Book, 1973.

Krippner, Stanley and Daniel Rubin. *The Kirlian Aura*. Doubleday Anchor, 1974.

Krupp, E.C. *In Search of Ancient Astronomies*. Double Day and Company, 1977.

Laird, Charlton. *Language in America*. Prentice Hall, Inc., 1970.

Mails, Thomas. *Fools Crow*. Doubleday & Co., Inc., 1979.

Montgomery, Ruth. *Strangers Among Us: Enlightened Beings From a World to Come*. Fawcett Crest Books, 1979.

_____. *The World Before*. Fawcett, 1977.

Moody, Raymond A. Jr. *Life After Life*. Bantam, 1986.

Moore, Gladys. *Forgotten Knowledge*. The Metaphysical Book Co., 1977.

Morgan, Henry Lewis. *Ancient Society*. Harvard University Press, 1964.

Morrison, Tony. *Pathways to the Gods--Mystery of the Andes Lines*. Harper & Row, 1978.

Muck, Otto. *Secrets of Atlantis*. Time Books, 1976.

Munzert, Alfred W. *Test Your IQ*. Monarch Press, 1980.

Nabokov, Peter. "America as Holy Land" (printed in *Americans Before Columbus*). Publication of the National Indian Youth Council, 1982.

"News from the World of Science" (printed in *Reader's Digest*). Reader's Digest, August, 1985.

Owens, Clifford, compiler. *A Story of Jesus, Based on the Edgar Cayce Readings*. A.R.E. Press, 1981.

Poignant, Roslyn. *Oceanic Mythology*. The Hamlyn Publishing Group Ltd., 1976.

Powers, William K. *Oglala Religion*. University of Nebraska Press, 1977.

Robinson, Lytle. *Edgar Cayce's Story of Origin and Destiny of Man*. Berkley Medallion Books, 1972.

Ross, Dr. Donald. "A Compendium of Thoughts." Unpublished, 1988.

Santesson, Hans Stefan. *Understanding Mu*. Warner Books, Inc. 1970.

Sims, Tom. "Lakota Oral Tradition," *Sinte Gleska College News*, Fall 1983 and Spring 1984.

Spangler, David. *Conversations with John*. Lorian Press, 1980.

Spino, Michael. *Beyond Jogging: The Inner Spaces of Jogging*. Celestial Arts, 1976.

Terrell, John Upton. *The Sioux Trail*. McGraw Hill Book Co., 1974.

"The Heat is On," *Time*, October 19, 1987.

"Three Wise Men and a Star" (printed from *Strange Stories, Amazing Facts*). The Reader's Digest Association, 1976.

Tompkins, Peter. *Mysteries of the Mexican Pyramids*. Harper & Row, 1987.

Toth, Max and Greg Nielson. *Pyramid Power*. Inner Traditions, 1985.

Vestal, Stanley. *Sitting Bull, Champion of the Sioux: A Biography*. University of Oklahoma Press, 1980 reprint of 1957 edition.

"Visitations of the Virgin," *Newsweek*, July 20, 1987.

Vitale, Barbara. *Unicorns are Real: A Right-Brained Approach to Learning*. Warner Books, 1986.

Von Daniken, Erich. *Chariots of the Gods*. Bern Porter, 1985.

_____. *Erich Von Daniken's Proof*. Bantam Books, London, 1977.

_____. *In Search of Ancient Gods*. G.P. Putnam & Sons, 1973.

Walker, James R. *Lakota Belief and Ritual*. University of Nebraska Press, 1980.

Waters, Frank. *Book of the Hopi*. Penguin, 1977.

_____. *Masked Gods: Pueblo and Navajo Ceremonialism*. Ballantine Books, 1963.

_____. *Mexico Mystique: The Coming Sixth World of Consciousness*. Sage Books, 1975.

Watts, Alan W. and Chung Liang-Huang. *Tao: The Watercourse Way*. Pantheon, 1977.

Zukav, Gary. *The Dancing Wu Li Masters*. William Morrow & Sons, 1979.

Zink, Dr. David. *Stones of Atlantis*. Prentice Hall, Inc., 1978.

ADDENDUM

For the past two years I have been producing videos on American Indian Prophecies. Video No.1 is basically a version of the chapter entitled Purification which is in this book. The only additions were comparisons by Nostradumus and Gordon Michael Scallion. Video No. 2 was a comparison and discussion on prophecies by Jose Arquelles, The Bible, Mayan calendar and the Quickening, the Great Pyramid of Giza as a calendar. Gordon-Michael Scallion and the Blue Star, Lakota story of the white Buffalo and the Blue Star. This video won an award at the Turtle Island Film Festival at Albany, N.Y. Video No. 3 was a review of the construction, purpose, and use of the Lakota sweat lodge. Presented were prophecies by Lakota Holy men Nicholas Black Elk, and Dawson No Horse. Also presented was the Wounded Knee Memorial Ride Prophecy. Video No.4 is entitled "Hale-Bopp, Comet or Star?" This comet is to become visible within the next month, so the information I had acquired had to be written very quickly. I called Susan Koyama, the Japanese translator for this book, and asked if there would be a possibility of including this addendum. She told me she was scheduled to review the final Japanese translation soon, so she said I needed to get the Addendum to her as soon as possible. The day I took the Addendum to her, she received the Japanese manuscript in the mail. It is also interesting to note that the moment I completed this Addendum I realized that the English edition of _Mitakuye Oyasin_ was scheduled for reprinting. Thus, the Addendum could be printed in the Japanese version as well as the English edition. Coincidence or synchronicity? The following is the written version of the 4th video of the American Indian Prophecy series.

HALE-BOPP COMET OR STAR?

For thousands of years, comets have been viewed as messengers of bad omens. But now modern science has helped us understand the nature of comets, so there is less superstition connected with comets today.

The head of the comet is called a coma: it is made up of frozen water and frozen gases. Comets are not visible, but when they get close to the sun they reflect the sunlight., giving them an appearance of being a bright object. As the comet begins to heat up because of the sun, gases escape from the head, causing dust particles to form around the comet. A tail of the comet is formed when the solar wind blows the fine dust away from the head. Depending on which direction the solar wind is blowing determines the direction of the tail. Sometimes a comet's tail will be in front of it. Comets follow orbits around the sun that tend to be oblong rather than circular.

The comet Hale-Bopp was discovered on July 23, 1995 by two amateur astronomers; Alan Hale and Thomas Bopp. Hale-Bopp was discovered 20 months from estimated time of arrival. Most comets are discovered 3 or 4 months out, so it is very large, estimated to be 40 kilometers in diameter. The comet originated in Sagittarius which here in America would be in the southern part of the sky. The calculated orbit for Hale-Bopp is 3,600 years. On July 23, 1996 Hale-Bopp split into two bodies, then rejoined itself 55 minutes later. Its brightness is above average for a comet. It is equal to Sirius in brightness. On March 23, 1997 Hale-Bopp will be closest to Earth, being approximately 123 million miles from Earth.

NASA observers saw a second body accompanying Hale-Bopp in October 1995; then they stopped releasing information pertaining to the comet. Amateur astronomer Chuck Shramek put a photo of the second body on the Internet and immediately a controversy erupted. Many have tried to discredit him, but Brian Marsden of Harvard, Smithsonian Center for Astrophysics, conceded there must be some non-gravitational forces at work to cause the comet to move as it does. Dave Allen talk show host on KSCO Santa Cruz, California stated that the number 23 appearing so often with Hale-Bopp is significant.

I decided to see what the I-Ching had to say about the number 23. The I-Ching is used for divination and is based on the law of synchronicity. In using the I-Ching a number is arrived at by tossing three coins. Heads equal the number 3 and tails equal the number 2. By tossing the coins and adding the numbers you determine a total number. For an odd number you draw a straight line and for an even number you draw a broken line. One does this six times, recording from the bottom up. To locate the proper hexagram on the I-Ching, one uses the top three lines for the top of the Trigram chart and the bottom three lines for the side of the chart. Where these two trigram intersect gives one the proper hexagram. This number is then referenced in the Book of Changes for understanding. The I-Ching is thousands of years old and is best explained by the psychologist Carl Jung's Principle of Synchronicity:

Synchronistic phenomena are attributed to the nature of archetypes. An archetype is said to be psychoid in character; that is, it is both psychological and physical. Consequently, an archetype can bring into consciousness a mental image of a physical event even though there is no direct perception of the physical event. The archetype does not cause both events; rather it possesses a quality that permits synchronicity to occur.

In referencing the number 23 Hexagram I found that it meant splitting apart. A friend of mine Howard Bad Hand of Taos, NM uses the I-Ching in his work. He told me that the 23rd Hexagram or "splitting apart" is symbolized by mountain over earth, also meaning light from the darkness. More synchronistic information on the number 23: each human embryo contains a pair of 23 chromosomes. So the number is connected to creation. The astrological ages are caused by the precession of equinox. This happens every 2300 years! We are just now leaving the Age of Pisces and are entering the Age of Aquarius. Is this coincidence or synchronicity? Lakota oral history states that we came from the Pleiades constellation and now I found that the Pleiades contain 2300 single stars.

What does the 23 enigma of Hale-Bopp really mean? Is there a second planet accompanying the comet? If so, how does this relate to the number 23 in the I-Ching and the number 23 in creation, and the number 23 in the next astrological age and finally the number 23 in the constellation Pleiades? Zechariah Sitchin believes that Hale-Bopp is the harbinger for a planet he calls the 12th planet. Sitchin, author of *The 12th Planet*, has the hypothesis that cosmonauts from the 12th Planet landed on Earth thousands of years ago and created man as a servant. He used the Sumerian texts and original Hebrew version of the Bible to support his hypothesis. Quoting from his book *The 12th Planet*, Sitchin says "For a long time, the expression The *Nefilim* were upon the Earth has been translated as 'there were giants upon the earth,' but recent translators, recognizing the error, have simply resorted to leaving the Hebrew term *Nefilim* intact in the translation. Also the verse 'the people of the Shem' must be taken in its original meaning 'sky ship.' What then does the term *Nefilim* mean? Taken from the Semitic Root, it means those who were cast down upon the Earth." Sitchin goes on to say, "Irrespective of the theological implications, the literal meaning of the verses cannot be escaped: the sons of the gods who came to Earth from heaven were the Nefilim and the Nefilim were the people of the Shem -- the people of the Sky Ships."

The reason Sitchin believes that Hale-Bopp is a harbinger for the 12th Planet is that both originated in Sagittarius and both have the same orbital return. Also according to his calculations, the 12th Planet caused the great flood during the astrological age of Leo (Lion); therefore, the Planet is due to return. Sitchin believes the 12th Planet is a couple of years behind Hale-Bopp.

From the book _The Pleiadian Mission_ by Randolph Winters, a Swiss farmer named Billy Meier had made contact with cosmonauts from the Pleiades. They told Mr. Meier that a comet had led them to our solar system thousands of years ago. Once on Earth they genetically created man from animal. From my research in _Mitakuye Oyasin_, "We are All Related" I found that Edgar Cayce stated that light beings created man from animal by using the endocrine system. This was done over a period of three generations. Cayce said that when man was created, a genetic code was put in him to keep the race pure, meaning man was to no longer have sex with animals. He was to have sex only with his race (man). Somehow, this code is misinterpreted by man today when he says the races should be white only or black only or red only.

The Pleiadians stated that the comet that led them to our solar system also caused the Great Flood 10,079 years ago. This is approximately the same time that Zecharia Sitchin estimated the Great Flood to have occurred.

The Pleiadians said that their mission is to show the real history of Earth and the real purpose for our lives. This is to be done by not interfering in our free will. The Pleiadians indicated that they came to the Pleiades from Lyra 300,000 years ago, then later came to our solar system, 227,000 years ago, settling on Earth, Mars, and Milona. Years later war broke out on Milona, totally destroying it. The huge blast pushed Mars out of orbit destroying all life there. It is interesting to note that in August 1996, NASA found signs of life on Mars.

The Pleiades made up of 2300 single stars is 500 light years from Earth. Six of the stars are visible from Earth and they form a little dipper. The star that forms the upper corner of the cup of this dipper is called Taygeta. Taygeta is the sun for the Pleiadians. Nine Planets orbit, their sun, one of which they inhabit and call Erra. In the book _Pleiadian Mission_ they discussed life on Erra. The following is a comparison of their life to the traditional Lakota life: language on Erra is mostly mental telepathy, with only a few spoken words. The Lakota believe in mental telepathy, especially those who participate in the ceremonies. In the Lakota language one word has many meanings. So it, like the Pleiadian language, has few spoken words. The government on Erra is composed of members called the High Council. They are elected and must be advanced spiritually. When making a decision members must be in 100% agreement or very close to it. Traditional Lakota council members had to prove they were sufficiently spiritual to be on the council by carrying a red hot rock without being burned. There were twelve members on a traditional council and when making a decision they had to be in 100% agreement. The economics on Erra is that of shared resources and respect for nature. Traditional Lakota society was also communal; those who were blessed to accomplish certain things shared that with those who could not achieve. This was done by using the giveaway system (see _Ehanamani: Walks Among_", by Dr. A.C. Ross for a more explanatory description). Traditional Lakota culture had a high respect for nature and all living creatures. This concept was also embellished into their ceremonies. Example: The word *Mitakuye Oyasin* is used after each prayer and it means "everything is related." Socially on Erra the Pleiadians are vegetarian, matrilineal, and believe in population control and reincarnation. The responsibility for raising children was shared by all. Before the Lakota acquired the horse and became the nomadic hunter, they were vegetarian and semi-carnivorous. Traditional Lakota believed in reincarnation, calling it "KINI". Traditional Lakota families believed in population control, having only two or three children per couple. Lakota families today still practice matriarchy and the raising of children to be shared by all, this is due primarily to the extended family structure which dictates that the mother's sisters are also the children's mothers. Is it coincidence or synchronistic that traditional Lakota life is the same as Pleiadian life? Pleiadians are humanoid and their features are much like ours. If one were to put street clothes on them and add a few cosmetics, one would not be able to recognize them. The Pleiadians encourage us to practice meditation. Meditation helps us learn to understand and control ourselves.

Since the Pleiades star system is 500 light years from Earth, the Pleiadians wanted to share how they are capable of traveling such great distances. They travel in what they call Beam Ships. Each has a diameter of 21 feet and weighs 1.5 ton. It is constructed of an alloy metal, some of which cannot be found on Earth. It has a two-drive system: first system propels up to speed of light, second system travels in hyper space. Beam ships operate telepathically from the Pleiadians via an organic computer. Each Beam Ship produces its own gravitational field from a light-emitting device which causes it to act like a planet. Travel from the Pleiades to Earth takes 7 hours. The first 3 1/2 hours are spent reaching hyperspace. Once this is achieved, the Beam Ship and the occupants dematerialize, become part of hyperspace and within a part-second they are within the Pleiadian system. The last 3 1/2 hours are spent "slowing down" and landing on Planet Erra (An example of how a Beam Ship dematerializes is as follows: an ice cube is a solid. When heat is applied it becomes liquid, when more heat is applied the liquid becomes a vapor. In each dimension the substance still contains the same properties.

The Pleiadians believe that Earth's humanity is on the verge of great changes, so they are here en masse to help us through these times.

In 1979, futurist Gordon Michael Scallion started having visions about Earth changes. His visions are 80% accurate. These are a few of Scallion's predictions which have come true:

1991 April and June   California earthquakes
1993 Blizzard of '93 in U.S.
1993 Mississippi River flood
1994 Hurricane Andrew
1995 Japan Earthquake (Kobe)
1995 Mississippi River flood
1996 Winter of '96, one of the coldest on record
1996 Year of space discoveries

He had a vision of the Blue Star appearing in the region of Orion's Belt. This star, at first would be thought of as a comet, then later be recognized as a star. Putti Kurtz stated in the Feb. 1997 issue of *Astronomy Magazine* that Hale-Bopp would travel north across the southern sky arriving at Orion's Belt in May, 1997. This area of the sky is also known as the heart of the White Buffalo constellation. Both Scallion and the White Buffalo legend state that this phenomenon would usher in a new era of unity, cooperation, and brotherhood. Scallion went on to state that people on Earth should become true partners with nature in order to assist the phenomenon. This can be done by taking a few minutes each day to observe the plant, birds, and animals. He also stated we could use meditation to

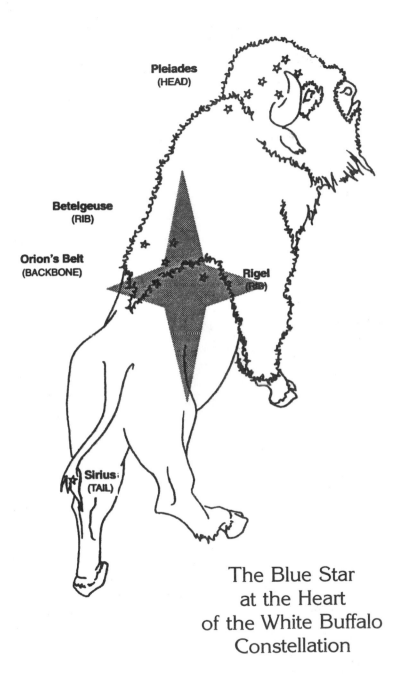

Pleiades
(HEAD)

Betelgeuse
(RIB)

Orion's Belt
(BACKBONE)

Rigel
(RIB)

Sirius
(TAIL)

The Blue Star
at the Heart
of the White Buffalo
Constellation

help ourselves achieve balance and harmony.

Hopi spiritual leader Dan Katchongva stated that if the races become separated from each other and no longer know their original teachings, the Creator would cause three world-shaking events to remind them that "we are all related." The story connected to the Hopi prophecy rock tells of a time when the Hopi emerged from the underground. The leading clans went in the four directions, then turned right, thus forming a Swastika symbol. The leading clans were: Fire, Spider, Eagle, Kachina, Bear, Badger, Flute, Snake.

The second group of clans which came out of the underground also went out in the four directions, then turned left, thus forming a Swastika in the opposite direction. These clans were named: Butterfly, Bluebird, Crow, Crane, Corn, Pumpkin, Sun, Lizard.

As the Hopi spread knowledge and information around the world, people would gradually become "two hearts," people who think with their head rather than their hearts.

Is it coincidence or synchronicity that the people of Earth today are left brain dominant? Left-brain dominant is to use rational thinking only versus the right-brain function of intuitive thinking. The Hopi prophecy rock goes on to show how man will reach a point where he can make a decision to either continue on the road of thinking with his head only or return to the road of thinking with his heart. If we continue thinking with our head only (rational), we will eventually destroy ourselves. If we take the road of thinking with our heart (intuition) we will eventually return to respect for nature and our survival. On the prophecy rock are also three circles which represent the three world-shaking (purifications) which are to remind us of our relativeness. Each of the shakings would be accompanied by a symbol. The symbol for the first shaking would be a "bug on a black ribbon being tossed into the sky." This was interpreted as an airplane. The time when airplanes were first used in war was World War I. So this was the first world shaking. The symbol for the second shaking would be when man used the Hopi migration symbol (Swastika) for war. This was in World War II. So this was the second world shaking. The symbol for the third world shaking would be the color red (a red covering or cloak). Will there be a World War III? The Hopi prophecy rock predicts the third shaking to be a time of total destruction or total rebirth. It is interesting to note that Nostradamus predicted World War III to start Jan. '91 and to last for ten years. The Hopi say that signs of the third shaking would be when :

    1. Trees will die (unknown disease kills palm trees in Florida).

    2. Man will build a house in the sky (sky lab?).

    3. Cold places become hot, and hot places become cold (global warming?)

    4. Land will sink, and land will rise(volcanos in Iceland cause new land?)

    5. There is an appearance of the Blue Star Kachina (Hale-Bopp?)

The Hopi say man needs to return to the original teachings if we want to survive the third world shaking. The following are ways to accomplish that.

The Hopi say we need to develop a respect for nature. Chief Seattle of the Suquamish, when asked by the government to sell the tribe's land, stated the following. These are excerpts from his speech which was titled, "How can one sell the air?"

We will consider your offer to buy our land.
Do not send men asking us to decide more quickly. We will decide in our time.
Should we accept, I here and now make this condition:
we will never be denied the right to walk softly over the

Blue Star
Kachina

grave of our fathers, mothers, and friends, nor may the
white man desecrate these graves.
The graves must always be open to the sunlight and the
falling rain.
Then the water will fall gently upon the green sprouts
and seep slowly down to moisten the parched lips of our
ancesters
and quench their thirst.

Every part of this earth is sacred to my people.
Every hillside,
every valley,
every clearing and wood,
is holy in the memory and experience of my people.
Even those unspeaking stones along the shore
are loud with the events and
memories in the life of my people.
The ground beneath your feet responds
more lovingly to our steps than yours,
because it is the ashes of our grandfathers.
Our bare feet know the kindred touch.
The earth is rich with the lives of our kin.

Men come and go,
like the waves of the sea.
A tear, a prayer to the Great Spirit,
a dirge (lament),
and they are gone from our longing eyes forever.
Even the white man,
whose God walked
and talked with him
as friend to friend,
cannot be exempt from the common destiny.

We may be brothers after all. We shall see.

The Lakota have included nature in their ceremonies and call this participatory spirituality (which is a form of meditation). Katchongva goes on to say that after the appearance of the Blue Star a "Mystery Egg" would hatch something new in global consciousness. Two possibilities immediately came to my mind. No. 1, both the serpent and the eagle come from an egg. They are symbolic of the duality in our would. The next root race will be androgynous., meaning the male and female personalities, within each person, will become balanced or whole. This event was prophesied by the Great Pyramid to happen starting in 1933 to 2033. The Pleiadeians prophesied the same change to occur starting in 1937 to 2030. In the book *Beyond Prophecies and Predictions* by Moira Timms, she states that "when humanity has entered into the new vibration related to the next evolutionary phrase, Christ's second coming will be seen by everyone in the world, but within an exalted state of consciousness." No. 2, The Pleiadians predicted that Earth would have contact with a Race of Beings from another planet in the year 2,000. These Beings are humanoid in feature and will arrive in giant spaceship the shape of an egg! The contact will take place in North America. Right now Mexico is the best candidate for the contact because of their high receptivity to UFO phenomenon. The Pleiadians will not make social contact with us until the year 2,300. Due to the tremendous gap in our spiritual and moral understanding, social contact with us at this time is simply not in their interest.

The Pleiadians state they are helping us evolve because they are our older brothers. Their mission on Earth is to show us our real history and purpose for our lives, but still allow us the free will decide whether to accept it or not. The Pleiadians contact individuals they know who could help serve their mission. This contact is done by mental telepathy. At this point I would like to share the story of my spirit guides, because their contact with me was via mental telepathy. In July 1958, I had a great vision, after attending a rodeo on an Indian reservation in South Dakota. We started home at sunset. In those days there were no electric lights at the rodeo, so when the sun went down it was over. It became dark as we were driving home through the Badlands. The road was gravel and very winding. As I came around a corner, I saw a telephone post stretched across the road. I hit the brakes and we bumped over the pole. No sooner had we run over it, than I realized it was not a telephone pole but a giant snake! Chills went right up my backbone. I hollered at my brother and cousins who were asleep in the car and told them what I had seen. I turned around and with the car headlights on, began looking for the snake. We were too scared to get out of the car. We continued looking for the snake but it was gone. I did not tell anyone about the incident because I felt no one would believe it. Twenty years later almost to the day I was on my first "Hanblecheya" or vision quest. Dawson No Horse was the holy man who had put me on the hill. On the first day I became hungry and thirsty; on the second day I was really thirsty, but I made it through the day. That night, I had a dream that was almost real. Three spirits came to me. They flew around me clockwise and stopped directly in front of me. They wore long robes and had no faces, but I received a really good feeling with their presence. It was like they were relatives but much more. One stood in front of the other two, who were behind his shoulders at each side. They spoke to me via mental telepathy, saying, "We want to communicate with you while you are here on Earth." I told Dawson this dream. He looked at me a short time, then said, "Study it Chuck, don't grab it and run," meaning there's a danger when one immediately thinks he or she is special, sacred, or spiritual based on one

The three spirits came to Dr. Ross
while he was on a vision quest.

dream or vision. Later I learned the names of the three spirits (angels). The word angel interpreted into English means spirit. The names of the three are as follows:

Angel of communication

Angel of god's beauty

Angel of fire(serpent) and freedom (eagle)

I asked my astrologer if there was a correlation between my astro chart and my dream. She said most definitely. She said "You are a Scorpio. The symbols for a Scorpio are the eagle, snake, and scorpion. You will be creative and Scorpios are usually designers, composers, writers. Your Mercury is mid-heaven which means you will be good at communication, speaking, or writing. Venus conjunct Neptune is the Beauty of God which means you will be creative, sensitive and have remarkable intuition. On your ascendent you are a cusp between Capricorn and Aquarius which means you have energy from both. Capricorn--leadership, Aquarius -- acceleration of spiritual awareness. Also your Sun is a cusp between Scorpio and Libra. Scorpio -- creativity and writing, Libra -- balance and harmony." So there is a direct correlation between my dream and my astro chart. (Coincidence or synchronicity?)

After I learned this, my thought immediately returned to what the Pleiadians had said. "They contact individuals who they know could serve their mission." My first book *Mitakuye Oyasin (We are All Related)* fulfills their mission. I have felt all along that the spirits were guiding me when I wrote the book. But are my spirit guides Pleiadian cosmonauts? The Pleiadians say they have contact with 17,422 people on Earth. The majority of these people are contacted via mental telepathy (dreams and visions). I remembered an author who stated she received information for her book from the Pleiadians. I quickly re-read the book which is titled *Bringers of the Dawn/ Teachings from the Pleiades* by Barbara Marciniak. In her book she stated that in March 1988 three Blue light beings had visited her. Next, she started receiving information from them via dreams, and as time went on she became more advanced spiritually, so she was able to have them speak through her. One of the messages from her book is that humanity is learning a lesson, that "everything is connected". In another book entitled _Close Extraterrestrial Encounters_ by Richard and Lee Boylan, I found this information -- The Boylans had researched 44 contactees with UFO beings and found 59% were positive encounters, 91% of the encounters were in a remote area. Dr. Boylan surmised that Native Americans are more likely to have contact with UFO beings because of their culture. In particular he noted the Hopi/Sioux. Several of the people interviewed stated they were visited by beings wearing hooded robes! Were the spirits who visited me on my vision quest actually Pleiadian cosmonauts? Is it coincidence that there is so much material supporting this theory of Pleiadian visitation or is it synchronistic? I don't want to be a two heart, so I would not disagree.

Ho Mitakuye Oyasin.

Ehanamani aka Dr. A. C. Ross
Denver, CO. Jan. 1997

ADDENDUM
BIBLIOGRAPHY

Boylan, Richard J. Ph.D. and Lee. *Close Extraterrestrial Encounters*. Wild Flower Press, 1993.

Chief Seattle. *How Can One Sell the Air?* Editors: Eli Gifford and R. Michael Cook, The Book Publishing Co. 1992.

"Hale-Bopp takes center stage", <u>Astronomy</u>, Feb. 1997.

Marciniak, Barbara. *Bringers of the Dawn*. Bear & Company, Inc., 1992.

Shramek, Chuck. His Website on the Internet. 1997.

Sitchin, Zecharia. *The 12th Planet*. Avon Press, 1993.

Timms, Moira. *Beyond Prophecies and Predictions*. Ballantine Books, 1994.

Winters, Randolph. *The Pleiadian Mission*. Gilliland Printing, Arkansas City, KS. 1994

VIDEO
MAIL ORDER FORM

American Indian Prophecy Videos I, II, II and Video on Hale-Bopp coment.

ORDER FORM			
Name _____			
Address _____			
City _____ State _____ Zip _____			

Qty	Title	Price/Video	Total
	VIDEO	$19.95 EA	
	SET (4 VIDEOS)	$59.95 EA	
		EA	
POSTAGE (BOOK RATE)			
	VIDEO	$ 3.95 EA	
	1 SET (4 VIDEOS)	$ 5.95	
	Handling ($1.50 per order)		$ 1.50
TOTAL			

Air Mail: For orders from outside the USA, add $5.00 per video. For orders from outside North America, add $8.00 per video.

Make checks, money orders and purchase orders payable to:
Wicóni Wasté – "Beautiful Life"
PO BOX 480005
DENVER, CO 80248
303-238-3420

CREDIT CARD ORDERS WELCOMED (VISA/MC)

BOOKS

ORDER FORM

Name _____

Address _____

City _____ State _____ Zip _____

Qty	Title	Price/Book	Total
	EHANAMANI		
	MITAKUYE OYASIN		
	SUBTOTAL		
	Postage (see below)		
	Handling ($1.50 per order)		
	TOTAL		

<u>Prices for both books</u>   <u>Postage (book rate)</u>

  1 copy $12.00 each   1-3 copies $ 1.50 per book

  2-10 copies   11.00 each   4 or more copies   .50 per book

11 or more copies   10.00 each

Air Mail: For orders outside the U.S., add $5.00 per book. For other international orders, add $8.00 per book.

Make checks, money orders and
purchase orders payable to: For wholesale orders, contact:

  Wicóni Wasté   Ingram Book Co.   (800) 937-8000
  PO BOX 480005   P.O. Box 3006
  DENVER, CO 80248   LaVergne, TN 37086-1986
  303-238-3420

CREDIT CARD ORDERS WELCOMED

ABOUT THE AUTHOR

Dr. A.C. Ross was named *Ehanamani* (Walks Among) in a Dakota ceremony. Ehanamani is a patrilineal family name. Great-Grandfather Artemus Ehanamani was put in prison at Fort Snelling, Minnesota after the eight-week war of 1862. Upon release, he went to Santee, Nebraska and joined his sister, my Great-Grandmother Maggie Ehanamani. Maggie married John Frasier and Artemus married John's sister. Because of the anti-Indian pressure at that time, Artemus and Maggie changed their names to Frasier.

The present Ehanamani (Dr. Ross) has worked for 27 years in the field of education as a teacher, principal, superintendent, college professor, and college department chairman. He has lectured on cultural understanding in 44 states in the U.S., 6 Canadian provinces, and 8 European countries. His second book, *Ehanamani "Walks Among"* is in the third printing.